GROWING ARTIFICIAL SOCIETIES

COMPLEX ADAPTIVE SYSTEMS
John H. Holland, Christopher G. Langton, and Stewart W. Wilson, advisors

Growing Artificial Societies

Social Science from the Bottom Up

Joshua M. Epstein
Robert Axtell

A product of the 2050 Project, a collaborative effort of the Brookings Institution, the Santa Fe Institute, and the World Resources Institute.

Brookings Institution Press
Washington, D.C.

The MIT Press
Cambridge, Massachusetts & London, England

Library of Congress Cataloging-in-Publication data:
Epstein, Joshua M., 1951–
    Growing artificial societies : social science from the
bottom up /
  Joshua M. Epstein and Robert Axtell.
        p.   cm.
    A monograph of the 2050 Project, a collaborative
effort of the Brookings Institution, the Santa Fe
Institute, and the World Resources Institute.
    Includes bibliographical references and index.
    ISBN 0-262-05053-6 (cloth). — ISBN 0-262-
55025-3 (pbk.). — ISBN 0-262-55026-1 (CD-ROM)
    1. Social sciences.   I. Axtell, Robert.
II. 2050 Project.   III. Title.
  H61.E67   1996
  300—dc20   96-25332
                                       CIP

                987654321

The paper used in this publication meets the minimum
  requirements of the American National Standard for
    Information Sciences—Permanence of Paper for
     Printed Library Materials, ANSI Z39-48-1984.

Typeset in Meridien and Helvetica

Composition by Automated Graphic Systems, Inc.
4590 Graphics Drive
White Plains, Maryland

Printed and bound by R.R. Donnelley and Sons Co.
Crawfordsville, Indiana

*Dedicated to
the memory
of our fathers*

Acknowledgments

For careful readings of the manuscript or portions thereof, for stimulating discussions, and for other contributions, we thank Henry Aaron, Philip Anderson, Brian Arthur, Jean-Pierre Aubin, Robert Axelrod, Mark Axtell, Robert Ayres, Steven Bankes, Aviv Bergman, Jill Bernstein, Bruce Blair, John Bonner, Steven Brams, David Campbell, John Casti, Nazli Choucri, Michael Cohen, Rob Coppock, Malcolm DeBevoise, Jeffrey Dean, Giovanni Dosi, George Downs, Samuel David Epstein, Hal Feiveson, Marcus Feldman, Duncan Foley, Walter Fontana, Cliff Gaddy, Murray Gell-Mann, David Golden, Valerie Gremillion, George Gumerman, Allen Hammond, John Hiles, John Holland, Bernardo Huberman, Yuri Kaniovski, Stuart Kauffman, Paul Kennedy, Alan Kirman, Ed Knapp, Chris Langton, Blake LeBaron, Axel Leijonhufvud, Rob Lempert, Simon Levin, Frank Levy, Robert Litan, Bobbi Low, Bruce MacLaury, Kati Mártinas, Gottfried Mayer-Kress, Jessica Tuchman Mathews, Geoff McNicoll, Greg McRae, John Miller, Cristopher Moore, Benoît Morel, M. Granger Morgan, Harold Morowitz, Bruce Murray, Kai Nagel, Tanvi Nagpal, Avidan Neumann, Scott Page, Alan Perelson, Robert Picard, David Pines, Steen Rasmussen, Dale Rothman, Thomas Schelling, Lee Segel, Elena Shewliakowa, Mike Simmons, Carl Simon, Herbert Simon, Robert Socolow, Paul Stares, Nick Vriend, Gérard Weisbuch, Arthur Wightman, Sidney Winter, and H. Peyton Young. For research assistance we thank Trisha Brandon, Alf Hutter, and Steven McCarroll. For administrative assistance we thank Ann Ziegler.

We are grateful to Robert Faherty for editing the manuscript. We thank Deborah Styles for editorial assistance, Julia Petrakis for indexing the book, and Natasha Hritzuk and Andrew Solomon for verifying the manuscript.

We are particularly indebted to John D. Steinbruner for his support, intellectual engagement, useful ideas, and wise counsel.

For their love and support we thank our families, especially our wives, Melissa and Roxanne, and our daughters, Anna Matilda and Emma.

We are very grateful to the John D. and Catherine T. MacArthur

Foundation for providing the grant that initiated the 2050 Project and to The Howard Gilman Foundation, Inc., for sustaining support. Funding for this book was provided by continuing grants from both foundations. Additional support for the project in its final stages was provided by The Pew Charitable Trusts. We acknowledge with great appreciation the interest and support of these foundations.

The views expressed in this book are those of the authors and should not be ascribed to the persons or organizations whose assistance is acknowledged or to the trustees, officers, or other staff members of the Brookings Institution or the other institutes that have collaborated in the 2050 Project.

Contents

Tables

Figures

Animations

CD-ROM Edition

A CD-ROM edition of *Growing Artificial Societies* is available. It operates on both Macintosh and Windows platforms and contains the complete text as well as the animations, which can be viewed in their entirety.

For ordering information, contact the Brookings Institution Press, 1775 Massachusetts Avenue N.W., Washington, D.C. 20036. Telephone: 202-797-6258 or 1-800-275-1447. Fax: 202-797-6004. E-mail: BIBOOKS@Brook.edu.

Introduction

Herbert Simon is fond of arguing that the social sciences are, in fact, the "hard" sciences.[1] For one, many crucially important social processes are *complex*. They are not neatly decomposable into separate subprocesses—economic, demographic, cultural, spatial—whose isolated analyses can be aggregated to give an adequate analysis of the social process as a whole. And yet, this is exactly how social science is organized, into more or less insular departments and journals of economics, demography, political science, and so forth. Of course, most social scientists would readily agree that these divisions are artificial. But, they would argue, there is no natural methodology for studying these processes together, as they coevolve.

The social sciences are also hard because certain kinds of controlled experimentation are hard. In particular, it is difficult to test hypotheses concerning the relationship of individual behaviors to macroscopic regularities, hypotheses of the form: If individuals behave in thus and such a way—that is, follow certain specific rules—then society as a whole will exhibit some particular property. How does the heterogeneous microworld of individual behaviors generate the global macroscopic regularities of the society?[2]

Another fundamental concern of most social scientists is that the rational actor—a perfectly informed individual with infinite computing capacity who maximizes a fixed (nonevolving) exogenous utility function—bears little relation to a human being.[3] Yet, there has been no natural methodology for relaxing these assumptions about the individual.

Relatedly, it is standard practice in the social sciences to suppress real-world agent heterogeneity in model-building. This is done either explicitly, as in representative agent models in macroeconomics,[4] or

---

1. Simon [1987]; the same point has been made by Krugman [1994: xi-xiii].
2. This is to be distinguished from the very different problem of determining what rules are actually employed by individual humans, a topic studied in experimental economics and other fields of behavioral science.
3. A recent statement of this basic concern is Aaron [1994].
4. Kirman [1992] makes this point forcefully.

implicitly, as when highly aggregate models are used to represent social processes. While such models can offer powerful insights, they "filter out" all consequences of heterogeneity. Few social scientists would deny that these consequences can be crucially important, but there has been no natural methodology for systematically studying highly heterogeneous populations.

Finally, it is fair to say that, by and large, social science, especially game theory and general equilibrium theory, has been preoccupied with static equilibria, and has essentially ignored time dynamics. Again, while granting the point, many social scientists would claim that there has been no natural methodology for studying nonequilibrium dynamics in social systems.

We believe that the methodology developed here can help to overcome these problems. This approach departs dramatically from the traditional disciplines, first in the *way* specific spheres of social behavior—such as combat, trade, and cultural transmission—are treated, and second in the way those spheres are *combined*.

"Artificial Society" Models

We apply *agent-based* computer modeling techniques to the study of human social phenomena, including trade, migration, group formation, combat, interaction with an environment, transmission of culture, propagation of disease, and population dynamics. Our broad aim is to begin the development of a computational approach that permits the study of these diverse spheres of human activity from an evolutionary perspective as a single social science, a *transdiscipline* subsuming such fields as economics and demography.

This modeling methodology has a long lineage. Beginning with von Neumann's work on self-reproducing automata [1966], it combines elements of many fields, including cybernetics (for example, Ashby [1956], Wiener [1961]), connectionist cognitive science (for example, Rumelhart and McClelland [1986]), distributed artificial intelligence (for example, Gasser and Huhns [1989]), cellular automata (for example, Wolfram [1994], Toffoli and Margolus [1987], Gutowitz [1991]), genetic algorithms (for example, Holland [1992]), genetic programming (Koza [1992, 1994]), artificial life (for example, Langton [1989, 1992, 1994], Langton *et al.* [1992], Brooks and Maes [1994]), and individual-based modeling in biology (for example, Haefner and Crist [1994] and

Crist and Haefner [1994]). However, there have been very few attempts to bring these literatures to bear on social science.[5]

The first concerted attempts to apply, in effect, agent-based computer modeling to social science explicitly are Thomas Schelling's. In a classic series of papers—"Models of Segregation" [1969], "On the Ecology of Micromotives" [1971a], and "Dynamic Models of Segregation" [1971b]—and later in the book *Micromotives and Macrobehavior* [1978], Schelling anticipated many of the themes encountered in the contemporary literature on agent-based modeling, social complexity, and economic evolution. Among other things, Schelling devised a simple spatially distributed model of the composition of neighborhoods, in which agents prefer that at least some fraction of their neighbors be of their own "color." He found that even quite color-blind preferences produced quite segregated neighborhoods.[6]

But Schelling's efforts were constrained by the limited computational power available at that time. It is only in the last decade that advances in computing have made large-scale agent-based modeling practical. Recent efforts in the social sciences to take advantage of this new capability include the work of Albin and Foley [1990], Arifovic [1994], Arifovic and Eaton [1995], Arthur [1991, 1994], Arthur *et al.* [1994], Axelrod [1993, 1995], Carley [1991], Danielson [1992, 1996], Gilbert and Doran [1994], Gilbert and Conte [1995], Holland and Miller [1991], Kollman, Miller, and Page [1992, 1994], Marimon, McGrattan, and Sargent [1990], Marks [1992], Nagel and Rasmussen [1994], Tesfatsion [1995], and Vriend [1995]. Additionally, computer scientists interested in questions of distributed artificial intelligence (DAI), decentralized decisionmaking, and game theory have been actively researching multi-agent systems. Important work here includes that of Huberman and coworkers (Huberman [1988], Huberman and Glance [1993, 1996], Glance and Huberman [1993, 1994a, 1994b], Huberman and Hogg [1995], Youssefmir and Huberman [1995]), Maes [1990], Miller and Drexler [1988], and Resnick [1994]. Biologists have even built models in which a population of agents representing humans exploits ecological resources (Bousquet, Cambier, and Morand [1994]).

In what follows we shall refer to agent-based models of social pro-

---

5. An important exception is Steinbruner's *The Cybernetic Theory of Decision* [1974].
6. Related work includes that of Vandell and Harrison [1978].

cesses as *artificial societies*.[7] In this approach fundamental social structures and group behaviors emerge from the interaction of individuals operating in artificial environments under rules that place only bounded demands on each agent's information and computational capacity. We view artificial societies as *laboratories*, where we attempt to "grow" certain social structures in the computer—or *in silico*—the aim being to discover fundamental local or micro mechanisms that are sufficient to *generate* the macroscopic social structures and collective behaviors of interest.[8]

In general, such computer experiments involve three basic ingredients: agents, an environment or space, and rules. A brief word on these may be in order before discussing the particular artificial society presented in this book.

Agents

Agents are the "people" of artificial societies. Each agent has internal states and behavioral rules. Some states are fixed for the agent's life, while others change through interaction with other agents or with the external environment. For example, in the model to be described below, an agent's sex, metabolic rate, and vision are fixed for life. However, individual economic preferences, wealth, cultural identity, and health can all change as agents move around and interact. These movements, interactions, changes of state all depend on rules of behavior for the agents and the space.

---

7. This term apparently originates with Builder and Banks [1991]; see also Bankes [1994].

8. So-called micro-simulation techniques, developed by social scientists at the dawn of the modern computer era, are philosophically similar to agent-based approaches insofar as both attempt to model social phenomena in a highly disaggregated way. An early pioneering work of this type is Orcutt *et al.* [1961], who wrote:

> Our socioeconomic system is a complicated structure containing millions of interacting units, such as individuals, households, and firms. It is these units which actually make decisions about spending and saving, investing and producing, marrying and having children. It seems reasonable to expect that our predictions would be more successful if they were based on knowledge about these elemental decision-making units—how they behave, how they respond to changes in their situations, and how they interact.

In comparison to agent-based modeling, micro-simulation has more of a "top-down" character since it models behavior via equations statistically estimated from aggregate data, not as resulting from simple local rules.

Environment

Life in an artificial society unfolds in an environment of some sort. This could be landscape, for example, a topography of renewable resource that agents eat and metabolize. Such a landscape is naturally modeled as a lattice of resource-bearing sites. However, the environment, the medium over which agents interact, can be a more abstract structure, such as a communication network whose very connection geometry may change over time. The point is that the "environment" is a medium separate from the agents, *on* which the agents operate and *with* which they interact.

Rules

Finally, there are rules of behavior for the agents and for sites of the environment. A simple movement rule for agents might be: Look around as far as you can, find the site richest in food, go there and eat the food. Such a rule couples the agents to their environment. One could think of this as an *agent-environment* rule. In turn, every site of the landscape could be coupled to its neighbors by cellular automata (see below) rules. For example, the rate of resource growth at a site could be a function of the resource levels at neighboring sites. This would be an *environment-environment* rule. Finally, there are rules governing *agent-agent* interactions—mating rules, combat rules, or trade rules, for example.

Object-Oriented Implementation

Contemporary object-oriented programming (OOP) languages are particularly natural ones for agent-based modeling. Objects are structures that hold both data and procedures. Both agents and environmental sites are naturally implemented as objects. The agent's data fields (its *instance variables*) represent its internal states (for example, sex, age, wealth). The agent's procedures (*methods*) are the agent's rules of behavior (for example, eating, trading). This *encapsulation* of internal states and rules is a defining characteristic of OOP and greatly facilitates the construction of agent-based models.[9]

---

9. For more on the software engineering aspects of artificial societies, see Appendix A.

Social Structures Emerge

Typically, we release an initial population of agent-objects into the simulated environment (a lattice of site-objects) and watch for organization into recognizable macroscopic social patterns. The formation of tribes or the emergence of certain stable wealth distributions would be examples. Indeed, the defining feature of an artificial society model is precisely that *fundamental social structures and group behaviors emerge from the interaction of individual agents operating on artificial environments under rules that place only bounded demands on each agent's information and computational capacity.* The shorthand for this is that we "grow" the collective structures "from the bottom up."

The Sugarscape Model

While the "bottom-up" approach to social science is quite general—as discussed at greater length in our concluding chapter—the primary focus of the present work is a particular instance of the artificial society concept that has come to be known as *The Sugarscape Model.* A brief summary of each chapter follows.

Life and Death on the Sugarscape

In Chapter II we introduce the sugarscape, a spatial distribution, or landscape, of generalized resource that agents like to "eat." The landscape consists of variously shaped regions, some rich in sugar, some relatively impoverished. Agents are born onto the sugarscape with a vision, a metabolism, and other genetic attributes. In Chapter II their movement is governed by a simple local rule. Paraphrasing, it amounts to the instruction: "Look around as far as your vision permits, find the spot with the most sugar, go there and eat the sugar." Every time an agent moves, it "burns" some sugar—an amount equal to its metabolic rate. Agents die if and when they burn up all their sugar.

A remarkable range of phenomena emerges from the interaction of these simple agents. The ecological principle of carrying capacity—that a given environment can support only some finite population—quickly becomes evident. When "seasons" are introduced, migration is observed. Migrators can be interpreted as environmental refugees, whose immigration boosts population density in the receiving zone, intensifying the competition for resources there—a dynamic with "national security" implications. Since agents are accumulating sugar at all times, there is always a distribution of wealth—measured in sugar—in the agent society. Does the wealth distribution mimic anything observed in human societies? Under a great variety of conditions the distribution of wealth on the sugarscape is highly skewed, with most agents having little wealth. Highly skewed distributions of income and wealth are also characteristic of actual human societies, a fact first described quantitatively by the nineteenth-century mathematical economist Vilfredo Pareto.[10] Thus we find the first instance of a qualitative similarity between extant human societies and artificial society on the sugarscape.

A CompuTerrarium

As a practical matter, if such highly skewed wealth distributions are immutable laws of nature, as some have claimed, then there is little hope of greater economic equity in society. A tool like Sugarscape can function as a kind of laboratory—a *CompuTerrarium*—where we alter agent behavioral rules, such as those governing trade or inheritance, in order to see how immutable this kind of distribution really is.

Agent Social Networks

Humans can be connected socially in various ways: genealogically, culturally, and economically, for example. Indeed, one of the things that makes humans complicated, conflicted, and interesting is that they can belong to many different communities, or social networks, at once. These networks change over time. And, most interestingly, group loyalties can come into profound conflict, as when brothers (members of a family group) fought each other (as members of competing political groups) in the American Civil War. One theme that runs through this entire book is *social connection*. In each chapter the local rules governing agent behavior permit us to define certain kinds of agent social networks. We represent such networks as graphs and track their evolution over time and space. In particular, Chapter II explores social networks of neighbors.

---

10. See Persky [1992] for an overview of the so-called Pareto law.

Up to this point, collective phenomena have emerged from interactions within a *single* population of agents. In Chapter III we "grow" distinct populations—cultural formations—of agents.

Sex, Culture, and Conflict: The Emergence of History

Indeed, the aim of Chapter III is to "grow" an entire history of an artificial civilization—a *proto-history*, as we call it. The storyline is as follows:

> *In the beginning, a small population of agents is randomly scattered about a landscape. Purposeful individual behavior leads the most capable or lucky agents to the most fertile zones of the landscape; these migrations produce spatially segregated agent pools. Though less fortunate agents die on the wayside, for the survivors life is good: food is plentiful, most live to ripe old ages, populations expand through sexual reproduction, and the transmission of cultural attributes eventually produces spatially distinct "tribes." But their splendid isolation proves unsustainable: populations grow beyond what local resources can support, forcing tribes to expand into previously uninhabited areas. There the tribes collide and interact perpetually, with penetrations, combat, and cultural assimilation producing complex social histories, with violent phases, peaceful epochs, and so on.*

This, then, is the social story we wish to "grow," from the bottom up. We will need a number of behavioral ingredients, each of which generates insights of its own.

The first ingredient of the proto-history is sexual reproduction. Like other rules that agents execute in the model, the "sex code" is completely *local* and very simple. Yet a rich variety of demographic trajectories is observed. For instance, populations—and population *densities* on the sugarscape—can fluctuate dramatically. Because mating is local, reproduction can cease and the population can crash if population becomes too sparse, or *thin*. Bottom up models such as Sugarscape suggest that certain cataclysmic events—like extinctions—can be brought on endogenously, without external shocks (like meteor impacts) through local interactions alone. Scientists have long been fascinated by the oscillations, intermittencies, and "punctuated equilibria" that are observed in real plant and animal populations. They have modeled these phenomena using "top-down" techniques of nonlinear dynamical systems, in which aggregate state variables are related through, say, differential equations. Yet we demonstrate that all these dynamics can be "grown" from the "bottom-up." And, when they are conjoined with the processes of combat, cultural exchange, and disease transmission, a vast panoply of "possible histories," including our proto-history, is realized on the sugarscape.

It is possible to *observe* evolutionary processes as they alter the genetic composition of our artificial society. For example, we expect that, over many generations, selection pressures will operate in favor of agents having relatively low metabolism and high vision. In fact, precisely this behavior emerges on the sugarscape. In Chapter III we assign a color to each agent according to its metabolism, then watch society change color as selection pressures "weed out" high metabolism individuals over time. Selection also operates on agent vision. There is a kind of genetic algorithm (GA) at work here, though we have not specified any "fitness function" beforehand. The topic of fitness, and the need to define it in coevolutionary terms, is addressed.

With a sexual reproduction rule in place, it is natural to study genealogy using social networks. It is very interesting to watch these "family trees" branch out across the sugarscape.

The next ingredient of the proto-history is tribe formation. How do tribes form? How does "social speciation" occur? To address these questions, we give agents cultural attributes and rules for their local transmission.[11] Cultural formations then "grow" from the bottom up. We represent cultural connections as lines between agents who have similar cultural attributes. These cultural connection networks expand, contract, and deform over time.

Finally, when agents of one cultural "tribe" encounter agents of a different tribe they may engage in a primitive kind of combat. That is, agents of opposite tribes may plunder one another for sugar. However, they are not so stupid as to attack agents who are capable of defeating them, or to attack an agent of a different tribe when there are others from that tribe in the vicinity who can retaliate successfully. Thus the combat rule results in agent movement patterns very different from the standard "eat all you can find" rule. We experiment with a variety of combat rules in Chapter III.

---

11. In Chapter IV we let economic preferences depend on these cultural attributes. Then, when cultural interchange and economic processes are both active, we have a model in which agent preferences change endogenously, in contrast to the assumption of fixed preferences standard in economic theory.

Sugar and Spice: Trade Comes to the Sugarscape

In Chapter IV a second commodity—"spice"—is added to the resource landscape, and each agent is given a corresponding metabolism for spice. The relative size of an agent's sugar and spice metabolisms determines its *preferences* for the two resources. The agents move around the landscape searching for those sites that best satisfy their preferences. Each agent must at all times possess positive quantities of *both* sugar and spice, or it dies.

Agents are then given the ability to trade sugar and spice. All trade is conducted in a decentralized fashion between neighboring agents, so-called bilateral exchange. Each pair of agents engaged in trade "bargains" to a local price and then exchanges goods only if it makes both agents better off. The main topics investigated in the chapter concern the relationship of local prices to the formation of a single "market-clearing" price and the welfare properties of these artificial markets.[12] These issues are investigated for two distinct classes of agents: the idealized economic agents found in economics textbooks and agents that are non-neoclassical insofar as they have finite lives and evolving preferences.

Markets of Neoclassical Agents

A crucial question is the following: *Under what conditions (for example, rules of agent behavior) will local prices converge to a market-clearing (general equilibrium) price?* We find that an equilibrium price is approached when our artificial society consists of a large number of infinitely lived agents having fixed preferences who trade for a long time. However, the resource allocations that obtain, although locally optimal, fail to be globally optimal. That is, there are additional gains from trade that our agents are unable to extract. The reason is that, while bilateral exchange is pushing the artificial economy toward a globally optimal configuration, production activities (resource gathering) are constantly modifying this configuration. These two competing processes—exchange and production—yield an economy that is perpetually out of equilibrium.

Because trade can simply be turned on or off in models of this type, we can study the effects of trade on other social variables. In particular, we find that the carrying capacity of the environment is *increased* when

---

12. On the notion of an artificial economy, see Lane [1993].

agents trade.[13] However, this salutary result does not come free, for under some circumstances trade increases societal inequality.

There are further implications for the welfare properties of markets. The "equilibrium" price that emerges under bilateral trade has a different character than the general equilibrium price of neoclassical theory; it is *statistical* in nature. One implication of statistical equilibrium is that agents having identical preferences and endowments can end up in very different welfare states through decentralized trade: they encounter different people, bargain to different prices, and trade different quantities, producing initially small differences in their respective welfare states, which may be amplified with time. This phenomenon is termed *horizontal inequality*.

Markets of Non-Neoclassical Agents

In neoclassical economic theory individual economic agents live forever and have fixed preferences. We give agents finite lives and the ability to reproduce sexually (as in Chapter III) and study the effects on economic behavior. The primary result of adding new agents to our artificial economy is to add variance to the distribution of trade prices in the sugar-spice market. This occurs because as new agents are born it takes time to have their internal valuations brought into line with those prevailing in the marketplace. The amount of price dispersion this effect produces increases as average agent lifetime decreases. Generally, increased variance in price corresponds to increased horizontal inequality, so the welfare properties of markets are further eroded by finite agent lives.

Preferences are permitted to evolve by coupling them to the cultural exchange process introduced in Chapter III. This yields several interesting economic phenomena. Agents whose preferences change from one period to the next find that their accumulated holdings—quite satisfactory in the previous period—may not satisfy their current wants, so they are more willing to trade than when preferences are fixed. Overall, we find that total trade volumes are larger with evolving preferences. Too, there is much more variation in prices under such circumstances, and the average price follows a kind of "random drift" process. Nothing like

---

13. In Chapter VI a set of Sugarscape model runs in which this phenomenon plays a crucial role is described. The evolutions of two societies, identical in all respects except that one engages in interagent trade while the other does not, are compared and contrasted. The nontraders end up extinct, while the traders are progenitors of a prosperous civilization.

the equilibrium of neoclassical theory emerges. Of course, the laissez-faire argument is precisely that markets, left to their own devices, allocate goods and services efficiently. The theoretical case for this is the so-called First Theorem of welfare economics. However, when markets fail to arrive at equilibrium, the First Welfare Theorem does not apply, and this case for laissez-faire is undermined.

Credit Networks

When agents are permitted to enter into credit relationships with one another very elaborate borrower-lender networks result. Agents borrow for purposes of having children. If an agent is of childbearing age but has insufficient wealth to produce offspring, then it will ask each of its neighbors in turn if they are willing to loan it the sugar it needs to become "fertile."[14] Prospective lenders assess the borrower's ability to repay a loan based on the borrower's past income. Once a loan has been consummated, it is repaid when due unless the borrower has insufficient accumulation, in which case it is renegotiated.

The credit connections that result from these rules are very dynamic. In order to study these relationships, graphs of creditor-debtor arrangements are shown in which each agent is a vertex and edges are drawn between borrowers and lenders. These graphs are updated each time period, thus showing the evolution of credit structures spatially. Unexpectedly, some agents turn out to be borrowers and lenders simultaneously, and this is most effectively displayed as a hierarchical graph, with agents who are only lenders placed at the top of the hierarchy and those who are only borrowers positioned at the bottom.

Social Computation

Yet another kind of social network is a trade partner graph, in which each vertex represents an agent and edges are drawn between agents who have traded with each other during a particular time period. Such graphs not only represent social relations but also depict the physical flow of commodities—sugar flows one way along an edge, while spice gets transferred in the opposite direction. These graphs—webs of economic intercourse—link agents who may be spatially quite distant, even though all trade is local, that is, between neighbors. These networks are

---

14. As we define this term in Chapter III, "fertility" includes an economic component.

ever-changing with time and are displayed in Chapter IV as animations.

During trade each agent acts to improve its welfare, that is, each participant optimizes its own utility function. A main question addressed in Chapter IV is: To what extent does individual (local) optimality result in overall social (global) optimality? Consider each agent to be an autonomous processing node in a computer, the agent society. *Individual agents (nodes) compute only what is best for themselves, not for the society of agents as a whole.* Over time, the trade partner network describes the evolution of connections between these computational nodes. Thus there is a sense in which *agent society acts as a massively parallel computer, its interconnections evolving through time.* This idea is fleshed out in Chapter IV.

Another important area where agent-based techniques apply very naturally is that of public health—epidemiology and immunology. We study this in Chapter V.

Disease Agents

Humans and infectious parasites have been coevolving for a long time. Certainly, it would be hard to overstate the impact of infectious diseases on human society. William McNeill [1976] has argued that infectious diseases played crucial roles in the spread of religions, political dominions, and social practices ranging from prohibitions on the consumption of pork to caste systems of the sort seen even today in India. In our own time, HIV has obviously had important sociopolitical impacts across a wide variety of groups on many continents. In light of all this, there is every reason to include epidemiology in social science. But there is equal reason to include social science in epidemiology! After all, the Black Death—*Pasteurella pestis*—could not have spread from China to Europe without human technological advances and commercial intercourse, notably in navigation and shipping. Needless to say, military conquest and migration have been equally efficient vehicles for the dissemination of infectious disease agents.

One aim of Chapter V, then, is to break down an artificial division between fields, presenting an adaptive agents model in which the spread of infectious diseases interacts with other social processes. We also hope to advance epidemiology proper, in several respects. First, our treatment of space differs fundamentally from that found in typical mathematical models. Also, mathematical epidemiology typically divides society into homogeneous subpopulations—compartments such as susceptibles and infectives within which there is no variation among individuals. In actuality, substantial variation exists; agents are heterogeneous precisely in that they have different immune systems. We endow every agent with its own adaptive immune system. Our immunology is, of course, very simple and highly idealized. Nonetheless, the explicit incorporation of an immune model into the epidemic model enriches and unifies the resulting picture. Important phenomena including immunological memory and the persistence of childhood diseases emerge very naturally. Moreover, since infected agents suffer a metabolic increase in our model, the epidemic dynamics affect (through the agents' metabolism-dependent utility functions) their movements and economic behavior.

A Society Is Born

Over the course of these chapters, the agents' behavioral repertoire grows to include movement, resource gathering, sexual reproduction, combat, cultural transmission, trade, inheritance, credit, pollution, immune learning, and disease propagation. In Chapter VI, we turn on all these dimensions and explore the complex, multidimensional artificial society that emerges. The book then concludes with a discussion of variations on, and extensions of, the current Sugarscape model.

Artificial Societies versus Traditional Models

Differences between our approach and certain other methodologies (for example, game theory) have already been noted. But additional ways in which artificial societies differ from traditional mathematical models and work in the field of artificial life (ALife) also merit review.

Heterogeneous Agent Populations

In a traditional ordinary differential equation model of an epidemic, the total population is divided into subpopulations of, say, susceptibles and infectives. These subgroups are *homogeneous*; nothing distinguishes one member from another. Similarly, in ecosystem models there are predators and prey, but homogeneity is assumed within each species. In macroeconomics the use of representative agents assumes away real-world heterogeneity.

By contrast, in agent-based models there is no such aggregation. The spatially distributed population is heterogeneous and consists of distinct agents, each with its own genetically and culturally transmitted traits (attributes and rules of behavior). Individual traits can change—adapt— in the course of each agent's life, as a result of interaction with other agents, with diseases, and with an environment. And, in evolutionary time (which can elapse quickly on computers), selection pressures operate to alter the distribution of traits in populations.

Space Distinct from the Agent Population

In *ordinary* differential equation models there is *no* spatial component at all. Susceptibles and infectives, predators and prey, interact in time but not in space.[15] In *partial* differential equation models there is a physical space **x**, but the state variables representing agent populations (such as the infection level) are continuous in **x**.

By contrast, in Sugarscape the agents live on a two-dimensional lattice, but are completely distinct from it. When diseases occur, they are passed from agent to agent, but the environment—and the agent's rules of interaction with it—affects the spatial distribution of agents, and hence the epidemic dynamics. Likewise, it affects the dynamics of trade, of combat, of population growth, of cultural transmission, and so on.

Agent-Environment and Agent-Agent Interactions according to Simple Local Rules

In the simplest form of our model agents are born with various genetic attributes, one of which is vision, and their rule of behavior is to look for the best unoccupied resource location. Their search is local; no agent has global information. Similarly, when we introduce trade there is no computation by any agent—or any "super agent" such as the Walrasian auctioneer—of a market-clearing price. Price formation takes place by a process of completely decentralized bilateral trade between neighbors. Under some conditions prices converge to a statistical equilibrium. This artificial economy stands in stark contrast to the neoclassical general equilibrium formalism, which relies on aggregate excess demand func-

---

15. These points apply with equal force to aggregate modeling of the system dynamics type (e.g., Stella, Dynamo).

tions—or some other form of *global* information—for the existence of and convergence to equilibrium.

Focus on Dynamics

One need not confine one's attention to equilibria, as is done in much of mathematical social science.[16] A social system's rest points, its equilibria, may be the most analytically tractable configurations, but it is by no means clear that they are either the most important or interesting configurations. Indeed, in much of what follows it will be the dynamic properties of the model, rather than the static equilibria, that are of most interest. In Chapter III, for instance, we study the dynamics of cultural transmission. Over thousands of time periods we see the sudden appearance of cultural "fads" and their irregular spatial propagation. These out-of-equilibrium dynamics seem far more interesting than the static cultural equilibrium into which the system is finally absorbed. With artificial societies built from the bottom up the transients are no more difficult to study than the equilibria.[17]

Beyond Methodological Individualism

Our point of departure in agent-based modeling is the individual: We give agents rules of behavior and then spin the system forward in time and see what macroscopic social structures emerge. This approach contrasts sharply with the highly aggregate perspective of macroeconomics, sociology, and certain subfields of political science, in which social aggregates like classes and states are posited *ab initio*. To that extent our work can be accurately characterized as "methodologically individualist." However, we part company with certain members of the individualist camp insofar as we believe that the collective structures, or "institutions," that emerge

---

16. Proofs of the *existence* of general economic equilibrium, *refinements* of equilibrium concepts in game theory (for example, Nash equilibrium), theories of equilibrium *selection* when multiple equilibria exist, and methods for evaluating the *stability* of equilibria are dominant themes in this literature.

17. When a model produces some interesting transient for which no explanation is immediately available, one can simply recreate the realization in question (by keeping track of seeds to the random number generators) and then glean data (noiselessly) from the agent population, data that will serve as the basis for analyses of the observed output. Or it may be useful to pause the model at some particular point in its execution and query particular agents for their state information.

can have feedback effects in the agent population, altering the behavior of individuals.[18] Agent-based modeling allows us to study the interactions between individuals and institutions.[19]

Collective Structures Emerge from the Bottom Up

A general equilibrium price, when obtained in our model, is an example of an emergent entity. In the usual general equilibrium story it is assumed that every agent "takes" a price issued from the top down, by the so-called Walrasian auctioneer. By contrast we "grow" an equilibrium price from the bottom up through local interactions alone, dispensing with the artifice of the auctioneer and the entire aggregate excess demand apparatus. Many other collective structures emerge in our artificial society: tribes of agents, stationary wealth distributions, and collective patterns of movement, for example.

Artificial Societies versus ALife

The Sugarscape synthesizes two "threads" from the ALife research tapestry. One is the field of cellular automata, or CA. A CA consists of a lattice of cells, or sites. At every time, each cell has a value, such as 0 or 1, black or white, "on" or "off," or a color selected from a set of colors, such as {red, blue, green}. These values are updated iteratively according to a fixed rule that specifies exactly how the "new" value of every site is computed from its own present value and the values of its immediate neighbors. Although, properly speaking, the pedigree of CAs extends at least as far back as von Neumann's work on self-replicating automata, the most familiar example is John Conway's game, "Life."[20] Cellular automata

---

18. Varying positions of methodological individualism are reviewed in Hausman [1992] and Arrow [1994].

19. The term "bottom up" can be somewhat misleading in that it suggests unidirectionality: everything that emerges is outside the agent. But in models with feedback from institutions to individuals there is emergence inside the agents as well.

20. The rules of "Life" are very simple:
   1. A cell in state 0 switches to state 1 if three of its eight lattice neighbors are in state 1; otherwise, it stays in state 0.
   2. A cell in state 1 stays in that state if two or three of its neighbors are in state 1; otherwise, it switches to state 0.
   3. Each cell is updated once per time period.

have been created as models of fluid flow [Doolen *et al.* 1990], earthquakes [Bak and Tang, 1989], clouds [Nagel and Raschke, 1992], forest fires [Bak, Chen, and Tang, 1990], biological systems [Ermentrout and Edelstein-Keshet, 1993], and a vast array of other complex *spatial* processes. The sugarscape proper—as opposed to the agents—is modeled as a CA.

Another major line of work in the ALife field does not involve an explicit space, but rather concerns the interaction of agents in a "soup"— a (space-less) environment in which each agent may interact directly with every other agent. The agents—unlike the cells in "Life"—have many different attributes (e.g., internal states and rules of behavior) which change through social interaction; see, for instance, Arthur [1994].

Sugarscape agents are very simple by design. In particular, we specify the agents' behavioral rules and watch for the emergence of important macro-social structures, such as skewed wealth distributions. The agents' rules do vary, but only parametrically, not structurally. For instance, every agent has a utility function. Culturally varying parameters enter into these utility functions, but the *algebraic form* of the utility function remains fixed, as does the agent's practice of *maximizing* the function. We say, then, that the microrules governing economic behavior adapt parametrically, not structurally. Similarly, agent immune systems adapt parametrically to new disease strains. The game in this particular research has been to design the simplest possible agents and explore what happens when they interact. As we shall see, the analytical challenges are already formidable. However, this is not the only possible game.

Instead of giving all agents the same rule, one might begin with a population of agents, each with a different rule, and allow selection pressure to change the rule distribution over time. In other words, no individual agent adapts, but (as in evolutionary game theory) those who prosper replicate and those doing poorly eventually die out. Over time, the rule distribution evolves. Society "learns" though individuals do not.[21]

Another modeling avenue is essentially to move the evolutionary process inside the agent. Here, each individual entertains a number of behavioral rules. Successful rules are promoted, while failures are

---

Under these rules a random initial distribution of black and white sites gives rise to a spectacular world of blinkers, wiggly "snakes," self-replicating "gliders," and stable structures on the lattice. For more on Life, see Sigmund [1993: 10–15, 27–39].

21. Examples of this approach in the context of the iterated prisoner's dilemma include Axelrod [1987], Miller [1989], and Lindgren [1992].

demoted, so that evolutionary learning occurs "within" the agent; Arthur [1994] is an example.

Yet more complex are models in which agents, in effect, "invent" entirely novel behavioral rules. Classifier systems (Holland [1992]) and neural networks (Rumelhart and McClelland [1986] and McClelland and Rumelhart [1986]) have been used in such models; see, for example, Marimon, McGrattan, and Sargent [1990] and Vriend [1995].

Cellular Automata + Agents = Sugarscape

In any event, if the pure CA is a space with no agents living on it, and the pure adaptive agents model represents agent kinetics with no underlying space, then the Sugarscape model is a synthesis of these two research threads. There is an underlying space—a "sugarscape"—that is a CA. But, populations of agents live on the CA.[22] The agents interact with one another *and* they interact with the environment. Interagent dynamics affect environmental dynamics, which feed back into the agent dynamics, and so on. *The agent society and its spatial environment are coupled.*[23]

Toward Generative Social Science: Can You Grow It?

The broad aim of this research is *to begin the development of a more unified social science, one that embeds evolutionary processes in a computational environment that simulates demographics, the transmission of culture, conflict, economics, disease, the emergence of groups, and agent coadaptation with an environment, all from the bottom up.* Artificial society–type models may change the way we think about *explanation* in the social sciences.

---

22. Other models in which agents inhabit a landscape include Holland's *Echo* [1992: 186–198], Ackley and Littman [1992], Yeager's *PolyWorld* (Yeager [1994], Wolff and Yeager [1994: 170–171]), and *BioLand* of Werner and Dyer [1994].

23. Heuristically, one thinks of an artificial society as a discrete time dynamical system in which the vector **A** of all agent internal states and the vector **E** of all environmental states interact as a high-dimensional discrete dynamical system of the general form:

$$\mathbf{A}^{t+1} = \mathbf{f}(\mathbf{A}^t, \mathbf{E}^t)$$
$$\mathbf{E}^{t+1} = \mathbf{g}(\mathbf{A}^t, \mathbf{E}^t)$$

where the vector functions $\mathbf{f}(\bullet)$ and $\mathbf{g}(\bullet)$ map the space of all states at time t to the space at $t+1$.

What constitutes an explanation of an observed social phenomenon? Perhaps one day people will interpret the question, "Can you explain it?" as asking "Can you *grow* it?" Artificial society modeling allows us to "grow" social structures *in silico* demonstrating that certain sets of microspecifications are *sufficient to generate* the macrophenomena of interest.[24] And that, after all, is a central aim. As social scientists, we are presented with "already emerged" collective phenomena, and we seek microrules that can generate them.[25] We can, of course, use statistics to test the match between the true, observed, structures and the ones we grow.[26] But the ability to grow them—greatly facilitated by modern object-oriented programming—is what is new. Indeed, it holds out the prospect of a new, *generative*, kind of social science.[27]

---

24. This usage of the term "sufficient" is similar to that of cognitive scientists Newell and Simon [1972: 13].

25. There may be many microspecifications that will do as well—the mapping from micro-rules to macrostructure could be *many to one*. In the social sciences, that would be an embarrassment of riches; in many areas, *any to one* would be an advance.

26. Issues of agent-based model validation—objectives, methods, and software tools— are discussed in Axtell and Epstein [1994].

27. On artificial societies and generative social science, see Epstein and Axtell [1996]. Further discussion of generative social science appears in Chapter VI.

Life and Death on the Sugarscape

In this chapter the simplest version of our artificial world is described. A single population of agents gathers a renewable resource from its environment. We investigate the distribution of wealth that arises among the agents and find that it is highly skewed. It is argued that such distributions are *emergent* structures. Other emergent phenomena associated with mass agent migrations are then studied. Social networks among neighboring agents are illustrated and their significance is discussed. Finally, it is argued that artificial societies can serve as laboratories for social science research.

In the Beginning . . . There Was Sugar

Events unfold on a "sugarscape." This is simply a spatial distribution, or topography, of "sugar," a generalized resource that agents must eat to survive. The space is a two-dimensional coordinate grid or lattice. At every point (x, y) on the lattice, there is both a sugar level and a sugar capacity, the capacity being the maximum value the sugar level can take at that point. Some points might have no sugar (a level of zero) and low capacity, others might have no sugar but large capacity—as when agents have just harvested all the sugar—while other sites might be rich in sugar and near capacity.

The Sugarscape software system (that is, the computer program proper) permits one to specify a variety of spatial distributions of levels and capacities. But let us begin with the particular sugarscape shown in figure II-1, which consists of 2500 locations arranged on a 50 x 50 lattice with the sugar level at every site initially at its capacity value.

The sugar score is highest at the peaks in the northeast and southwest quadrants of the grid—where the color is most yellow—and falls off in a series of terraces.[1] The sugar scores range from some maximum—

---

1. Terms like "peak" or "mountain" are not used to suggest physical elevation, but to denote regions of high sugar level.

Figure II-1. A Sugarscape   **Figure II-2.** Sugarscape with Agents

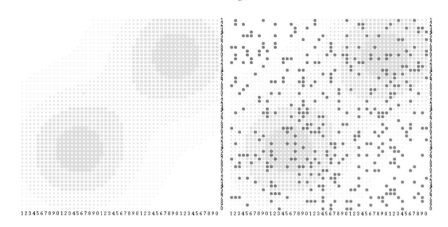

here 4—at the peaks to zero at the extreme periphery. The sugarscape wraps around from right to left (that is, were you to walk off the screen to the right, you would reappear at the left) and from top to bottom, forming a doughnut—technically, a torus.

Simple Local Rules for the Environment

In our model, autonomous agents inhabit this sugarscape and constantly collect and consume sugar. We therefore need to postulate a rule for how the sugar regenerates—how it grows back after it is harvested by the agents.

Various rules are possible.[2] For instance, sugar could grow back instantly to its capacity. Or it could grow back at a rate of one unit per time step. Or it could grow back at different rates in different regions of the sugarscape. Or the growback rate might be made to depend on the sugar level of neighboring sites. We will examine several of these possibilities. To begin, however, we stipulate that at *each lattice point* the sugarscape obeys the following simple rule:

---

2. The main constraint we impose on ourselves in constructing such rules throughout this book is to make them as simple as possible. This has two main implications, one theoretical and one practical. Theoretically, rule simplicity suggests that the agents use only local information. Practically, we want to be able to state a particular rule in just a few lines of code.

Sugarscape growback rule G_α: At each lattice position, sugar grows back at a rate of α units per time interval up to the capacity at that position.[3]

With the sugarscape described, we now "flesh out" what we mean by "agents."

The Agents

Just as there is an initial distribution of sugar, there is also an initial population of "agents." We want to give these agents the ability to move around the sugarscape performing various tasks. In this chapter they simply gather sugar and eat it.[4] In later chapters their behavioral repertoire expands to include sex, cultural exchange, combat, trade, disease transmission, and so on. These actions require that each agent have internal states and behavioral rules.[5] We describe these in turn.

Agent States

Each agent is characterized by a set of fixed and variable states. For a particular agent, its genetic characteristics are fixed for life while its wealth, for instance, will vary over time.

One state of each agent is its location on the sugarscape. At every time each agent has a position given by an ordered pair (x, y) of horizontal and vertical lattice coordinates, respectively. Two agents are not allowed to occupy the same position. Some agents are born high on the sugarscape near the peaks of the sugar mountains shown in figure II-1. Others start out in the sugar "badlands" where sugar capacities are very low. One might think of an agent's initial position as its "environmental endowment." We shall first investigate a random distribution of 400 agents, as shown in figure II-2.

Each agent has a genetic endowment consisting of a sugar metabolism

---

3. The rule can be stated formally. Call the current resource (sugar) level r^t and the capacity c. Then the new resource level, r^{t+1}, is given by
$$r^{t+1} = min(r^t + \alpha, c).$$

4. For a similar model, see Packard's [1989] artificial ecology.

5. As noted in Chapter I, each agent is implemented as an "object"; its internal states are its "instance variables," while its behavioral rules are specified by its "methods." Technically, the states of an agent are data while its behavioral rules are procedures (or subroutines).

Figure II-3. Agent Vision

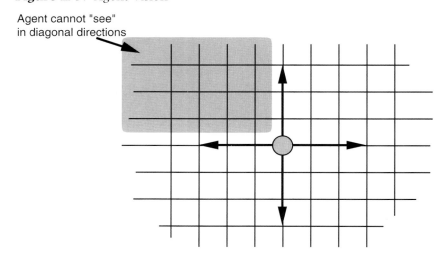

Agent cannot "see"
in diagonal directions

and a level of vision. Agents have different values for these genetic attributes; thus the agent population is *heterogeneous.*[6]

The agent's metabolism is simply the amount of sugar it burns per time step, or iteration. Metabolisms are randomly distributed across agents. For the runs of the model described immediately below, metabolism is uniformly distributed with a minimum of 1 and a maximum of 4.

Agent vision is also randomly distributed. Agents with vision v can see v units in the four principal lattice directions: north, south, east, and west. Agents have no diagonal vision. This lack of diagonal vision is a form of imperfect information and functions to bound the agents' "rationality," as it were. The nature of agent vision is illustrated in figure II-3. An agent with vision 3 can look out 3 units in the principal lattice directions. In what follows vision is initially distributed uniformly across agents with values ranging from 1 to 6, unless stated otherwise.

All agents are given some initial endowment of sugar, which they carry with them as they move about the sugarscape. Sugar collected but not eaten—what an agent gathers beyond its metabolism—is added to the agent's sugar holdings.[7] There is no limit to how much sugar an individual agent may accumulate.

---

6. When the number of genetic attributes is large it may even be the case that no two agents are genetically identical.

7. Agent holdings do not decay over time.

Simple Local Rules for the Agents

The agents are also given a movement rule. Movement rules process local information about the sugarscape and return rank orderings of the sites according to some criterion. Such rules are called "movement rules" since each agent moves to the site it ranks highest. As with the sugarscape growback rule, we require that agent movement be governed by a *simple* rule.

A natural way to order the sites is by the amount of sugar present at each site within an agent's vision. This results in the following movement rule, which is a kind of gradient search algorithm:

Agent movement rule **M**:
- Look out as far as vision permits in the four principal lattice directions and identify the unoccupied site(s) having the most sugar;[8]
- If the greatest sugar value appears on multiple sites then select the nearest one;[9]
- Move to this site;[10]
- Collect all the sugar at this new position.

Succinctly, rule **M** amounts to this: From all lattice positions within one's vision, find the nearest unoccupied position of maximum sugar, go there and collect the sugar.[11]

At this point the agent's accumulated sugar wealth is *incremented* by the sugar collected and *decremented* by the agent's metabolic rate. If at any time the agent's sugar wealth falls to zero or below—that is, it has been unable to accumulate enough sugar to satisfy its metabolic demands—then we say that the agent has starved to death and it is removed from the sugarscape. If an agent does not starve it lives forever.

---

8. The order in which each agent searches the four directions is random.

9. That is, if the largest sugar within an agent's vision is four, but the value occurs twice, once at a lattice position two units away and again at a site three units away, the former is chosen. If it appears at multiple sites the same distance away, the first site encountered is selected (the site search order being random).

10. Notice that there is no distinction between how far an agent can move and how far it can see. So, if vision equals 5, the agent can move up to 5 lattice positions north, south, east, or west.

11. Since all agents follow this behavioral rule, there is a sense in which they are quite homogeneous. However, recalling that vision is randomly distributed in the agent population, two distinct agents placed in identical environments will not generally respond (behave) in the same way, that is, move to the same location.

Each agent is permitted to move once during each artificial time period. The order in which agents move is randomized each time period.[12]

Artificial Society on the Sugarscape

All the ingredients are now in hand. We have a sugarscape and an initial population of agents, each of whom comes into the world with an environmental and genetic endowment, and we have simple behavioral rules for the sugarscape and the agents. Initially there will be only one rule for the agents and one for the sugarscape, but in subsequent chapters both the environment and the agents will execute multiple rules.[13] So a notation is needed to describe the rules being executed for any particular run of the model. Call **E** the set of rules that the environment executes, and let **A** be the set of rules the agents follow. Then the ordered pair (**E**, **A**) is the complete set of rules.

For the first run of the model, the sugarscape will follow an instance of the general rule, G_α, that we call the "immediate growback rule."

Sugarscape rule G_∞: Grow back to full capacity immediately.[14]

This rule says that no matter what the current sugar level is at a site, replace it with that site's sugar capacity. The agents will all execute movement rule **M**. Thus the complete set of rules being executed is $(\{G_\infty\}, \{M\})$.

Can you guess what will happen for these rules? Will the agents all clump together atop the sugar mountains? Will agent motion persist indefinitely? Actual dynamics are shown in animation II-1.[15]

What is striking to us is the way the agents ultimately "stick" to the

---

12. All results reported here have been produced by running the model on a serial computer; therefore only one agent is "active" at any instant. In principle, the model could be run on parallel hardware, permitting agents to move simultaneously (although **M** would have to be supplemented with a conflict resolution rule to handle cases in which two or more agents simultaneously decide to inhabit the same site). Whenever one simulates on a serial machine processes that occur in parallel, it is important to randomize the agent order periodically to ensure against the production of simulation artifacts [Huberman and Glance, 1993].

13. Appendix B presents a summary statement of all rules used, in their most general form.

14. Under the definition of G_α, G_∞ ensures that sites grow back instantly to capacity, since

$$r^{t+1} = \min(\infty, c) = c.$$

15. Users wishing to view animations should consult the README file on the CD-ROM for instructions.

Animation II-1. Societal Evolution under Rules ($\{\mathbf{G}_\infty\}$, $\{\mathbf{M}\}$) from a Random Initial Distribution of Agents

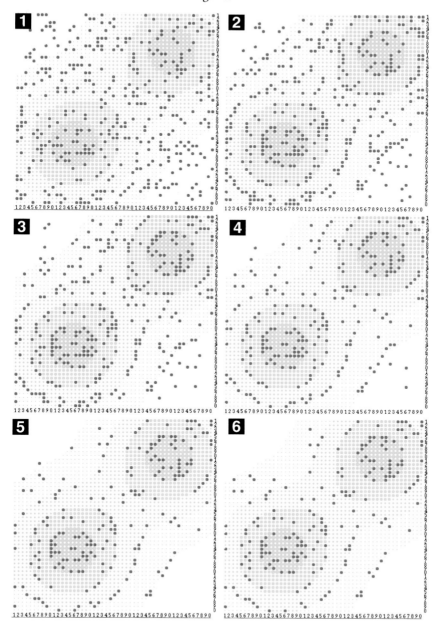

ridges of the terraced sugarscape. With immediate growback to capacity, the agents' limited vision explains this behavior. Specifically, suppose you are an agent with vision 2 and you are born on the terrace of sugar height 2, just one unit south of the sugar terrace of level 3. With vision 2, you can see that the nearest maximum sugar position is on the ridge of the sugar terrace of height 3, so, obeying rule **M**, you go there and collect the sugar. Since there is instant growback, no point *on* the level 3 sugar terrace is an *improvement*; and with vision of only 2, you cannot see the higher terrace of sugar level 4. So you stick on the ridge.

Also notice that some agents die. For those with high metabolism *and* low vision, life is particularly hard. This run of the model reaches a steady-state configuration once these unfortunates have died and the rest have attained the best positions they can find.[16] Much richer dynamics result if we slow down the rate at which the sugarscape regenerates, as shown in the next run of our artificial society.

For this second run we again take the initial population to be 400 agents arranged in a random spatial distribution. Each agent again executes rule **M**. But now let us change the sugarscape rule to G_1: Every site whose level is less than its capacity grows back at 1 unit per time period. The complete rules are then $(\{G_1\}, \{M\})$. The evolution is shown in animation II-2.

What first catches the eye in this animation is the continuous buzz of activity; it reminds one of "hiving." But it is both purposeful and efficient. It is purposeful in that the agents concentrate their activities on the sugar peaks. Indeed, two "colonies" seem to form, one on each mountain. If the intervening desert (low sugar zone) between the main

---

16. Each time the model is run under rules $(\{G_\infty\}, \{M\})$, results qualitatively similar to those of animation II-1 are produced. However, because the initial population of agents is random—each agent has genetics and initial location drawn from certain probability distribution functions—runs made with different streams of random numbers will generally be completely different microscopically, that is, at the level of the agents. (Distinct random number streams are created from run to run either by using distinct seeds in a fixed random number generator (RNG) or by employing altogether different RNGs. A common way to make successive random number seeds uncorrelated in consecutive runs of a model is to tie them to something independent of the model, such as the actual time at which the user starts the run.) Because the search direction in rule **M** is stochastic, even runs having identical populations of agents will differ at the micro-level when, for example, a RNG is re-seeded in the course of a run. All this said, however, let us emphasize that any particular run of the model is completely reproducible. That is, when the sequence of random numbers is specified *ex ante* the model is deterministic. Stated yet another way, model output is invariant from run to run when all aspects of the model are kept constant, including the stream of random numbers.

Animation II-2. Societal Evolution under Rules ($\{\mathbf{G}_1\}$, $\{\mathbf{M}\}$) from a Random Initial Distribution of Agents

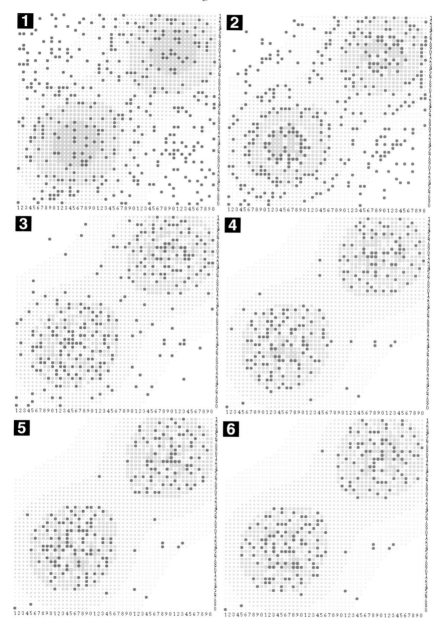

sugar mountains were widened, the spatial segregation seen here would be even more pronounced.

The agents are also efficient grazers. Focusing your attention on a particular sugar location atop one of the sugar peaks, you will see that once it attains some level near its capacity value, it is struck. Then the agent moves away, leaving a white site. Once the site grows back, some agent will zip over and hit it, and so it goes.

An alternative view of rule **M** is that it is a *decentralized* harvesting rule. Specifically, imagine yourself to be the owner of the sugarscape resources and that your goal is to harvest as much sugar as possible. You could give each of your agents explicit instructions as to which site to harvest at what time. Such a harvesting program could turn out to be very complicated indeed, especially when the differential capabilities of the agents are taken into account. But **M** is also a harvesting program, a highly decentralized one.

Carrying Capacity

This simulation illustrates one of the fundamental ideas in ecology and environmental studies—the idea of a *carrying capacity*: A given environment will not support an indefinite population of agents.[17] In this case, although 400 agents begin the simulation, a carrying capacity of approximately 224 is eventually reached. This is revealed in the time series of agent population given in figure II-4.

We can systematically study the dependence of the carrying capacity on the genetic composition of the agent population. To do this one simply specifies particular distributions of vision and metabolism among the agents and lets the model evolve until the asymptotic population level—the carrying capacity—is reached. For a given set of distributions, each run of the model will produce a somewhat different population value, due to stochastic variations, hence, multiple runs must be performed. Figure II-5 gives the dependence of carrying capacity on inital mean vision, parameterized by initial mean metabolism, <m>, starting with 500 agents.[18]

As agent vision increases each agent can see more of the sugarscape and is therefore a more efficient harvester. Similarly, as agent metabolism decreases, each agent finds it somewhat easier to survive.

---

17. For a comprehensive and considered inquiry into the question of Earth's human carrying capacity, see Cohen [1995].

18. Each data point represents the mean value of 10 runs.

Figure II-4. Time Series of Population under Rules ($\{\mathbf{G}_1\}$, $\{\mathbf{M}\}$) from a Random Initial Distribution of Agents; Asymptotic Approach to the Environmental Carrying Capacity of 224

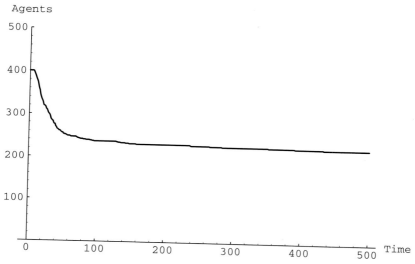

Figure II-5. Carrying Capacities as a Function of Mean Agent Vision, Parameterized by Metabolism, under Rules ($\{\mathbf{G}_1\}$, $\{\mathbf{M}\}$) from a Random Initial Distribution of Agents

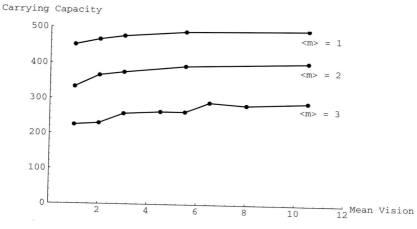

Selection without Sex

In a primitive form our artificial world also illustrates a central idea of evolutionary theory, that of *selection*. As mentioned above, at the outset metabolism and vision are randomly distributed across agents, with each varying between some minimum and maximum value. However, by the time the carrying capacity is attained, the population is skewed in favor of agents with low metabolism and high vision. These agents enjoy a selective advantage over the high metabolism, low vision agents. And as we shall see in the next chapter, when we add sexual reproduction to the agents' behavioral repertoire, this process becomes accretive generationally, producing much stronger tendencies toward agents who are increasingly "fit." Even without sex, selection pressures can be substantial. In the run depicted in animation II-2, the initial mean vision and metabolism were 3.5 and 2.5, respectively. After 500 time periods, selection had increased mean vision to 4.1 and reduced mean metabolism to 1.8.

Wealth and Its Distribution in the Agent Population

All the while in our artificial world agents are accumulating wealth (measured, of course, in sugar). And so, at any time, there is a distribution of wealth in society. The topic of wealth distribution has always interested economists. To study the distribution of wealth in our artificial society we need to modify the previous run in two related ways. First, if agents are permitted to live forever then no stationary wealth distribution ever obtains—the agents simply accumulate indefinitely. Since death is indisputably a fact of life, it is only realistic to insist on finite agent lifetimes. So we set each agent's maximum achievable age—beyond which it cannot live—to a random number drawn from some interval [a,b]. Of course, agents can still die of starvation, as before.

Given that agents are to have finite lifetimes, the second modification that must be implemented is a rule of agent replacement. One can imagine many such rules; for example, a fixed number of new agents could be added each period. However, to ensure a stationary wealth distribution it is desirable to use a replacement rule that produces a constant population. The following replacement rule achieves this goal.

> <u>Agent replacement rule $\mathbf{R}_{[a,b]}$</u>: When an agent dies it is replaced
> by an agent of age 0 having random genetic attributes, random

position on the sugarscape, random initial endowment, and a maximum age randomly selected from the range [a,b].

To study the actual evolution of the distribution of wealth on the sugarscape we place 250 agents—approximately the carrying capacity—randomly about the sugarscape and let them move and accumulate sugar as before (agent movement rule **M**). Replacement rule $\mathbf{R}_{[60,\ 100]}$ is in effect.[19] Initial agent endowments are uniformly distributed between 5 and 25. The sugarscape grows back at unit rate (environment rule $\mathbf{G}_1$). Now, since we want to track the distribution of wealth, not the spatial distribution of agents, we show a histogram of wealth animated over time. In animation II-3, the horizontal axis gives the range of individual wealth in society, divided into ten "bins." The vertical axis gives the number of agents falling into the various bins. How does the distribution evolve?

While initially quite symmetrical, the distribution ends up highly skewed.[20] Such skewed wealth distributions are produced for wide ranges of agent and environment specifications. They seem to be characteristic of heterogeneous agents extracting resources from a landscape of fixed capacity. By contrast, the distribution of *income*, defined as the amount harvested per period less metabolism, is much less skewed.[21]

Emergence

In the sciences of complexity, we would call this skewed distribution an *emergent structure*, a stable macroscopic or aggregate pattern induced by the local interaction of the agents. Since it emerged "from the bottom up," we point to it as an example of *self-organization*. Left to their own, strictly local, devices the agents achieve a *collective* structuring of some sort. This distribution is our first example of a so-called *emergent structure*.

The term "emergence" appears in certain areas of complexity theory, distributed artificial intelligence, and philosophy. It is used in a variety of ways to describe situations in which the interaction of many autonomous individual components produces some kind of coherent, systematic behavior involving multiple agents. To our knowledge, no

---

19. Note that the mean death age will be 80 when few agents die of starvation.

20. Agents having wealth above the mean frequently have both high vision and low metabolism. In order to become one of the very wealthiest agents one must also be born high on the sugarscape and live a long life.

21. The maximum income possible is 3, since the maximum sugar level is 4 and the minimum metabolism is 1.

Animation II-3. Wealth Histogram Evolution under Rules ($\{\mathbf{G}_1\}$, $\{\mathbf{M}$, $\mathbf{R}_{[60,100]}\}$) from a Random Initial Distribution of Agents

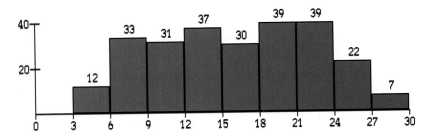

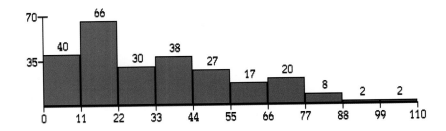

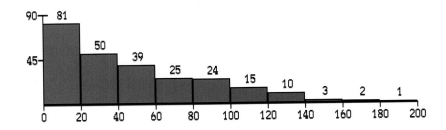

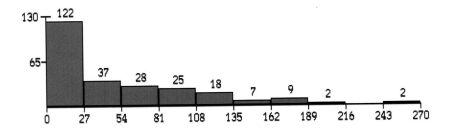

completely satisfactory *formal* theory of "emergence" has been given.[22] A particularly loose usage of "emergent" simply equates it with "surprising" or "unexpected," as when researchers are unprepared for the kind of systematic behavior that emanates from their computers.[23] A less subjective usage applies the term to group behaviors that are qualitatively different from the behaviors of individuals composing the group.

We use the term "emergent" to denote *stable macroscopic patterns arising from the local interaction of agents*. One example is the skewed wealth distribution; here, the emergent structure is statistical in nature. There is a qualitatively different type of emergent phenomenon that we also observe. An example of this, described below, occurs when a wave of agents moves collectively in a diagonal direction on the sugarscape, this even though individual agents can move only north, south, east, or west. That is, the group adopts a heading unavailable to any individual! While both the highly skewed wealth distribution and the collective wave satisfy our definition of emergence, they differ in a fundamental respect. We know what it would *mean* for an individual agent to travel on a diagonal; the local rule simply prohibits it. By contrast, we do not know what it would *mean* for an individual to have a wealth distribution; at a given time, only groups can have distributions.[24]

Understanding how simple local rules give rise to collective structure is a central goal of the sciences of complexity. As we will frequently observe, such understanding would have fundamental implications for policy. For instance, we might be able to distinguish conditions (on information or spatial heterogeneity, for example) conducive to the emergence of efficient markets from conditions making their emergence highly unlikely. We might then be better equipped to answer the following sort of question: Is it reasonable to base policy on the assumption that if central authorities "just get out of the way" then efficient markets will self-organize in Russia? Clearly, implicit assumptions on seemingly

---

22. Interesting efforts are under way, however; see Baas [1994].

23. This usage obviously begs the question, "Surprising to whom?"

24. To formalize things somewhat, let A denote an agent and C denote a collection of agents. Let P(A) denote the proposition "A has property P," and likewise for P(C). Then there are at least two types of emergence:

1. P(A) and P(C) are both meaningful, but only P(C) is observed (for example, collective diagonal waves);

2. Only P(C) is meaningful and it is observed (for example, the skewed wealth distribution).

abstract questions of "emergence" drive policy at fundamental levels.

Returning to the wealth distribution of animation II-3, some have argued, especially in the context of the so-called Pareto "law," that highly skewed distributions of income and wealth represent some sort of "natural order," a kind of immutable "law of nature."[25] Artificial social systems let us explore just how immutable such distributions are. We can adjust *local* rules—like those concerning inheritance and taxation—and see if the same *global* pattern in fact emerges.

Measures of Economic Inequality: The Gini Coefficient

It is possible to fit the wealth distribution of animation II-3, or its cumulative distribution counterpart, to any number of empirically significant distribution functions. Such distributions—the Pareto-Levy distribution being perhaps the best known—are typically characterized by one or two parameters, and it might be informative to compare the parameter values obtained from our artificial society with those from real societies. The point of such exercises is to compress information on whole distributions into just a few parameters. This not only facilitates comparison with real economic data but also provides a basis for describing the results of simulations in summary terms. For example, if rules $(\mathbf{E}, \mathbf{A})$ yield a wealth distribution statistic S while rules $(\mathbf{E}, \mathbf{A}')$ result in $S' > S$, it can unambiguously be said that changing agent rules from $\mathbf{A}$ to $\mathbf{A}'$ causes S to increase.

In particular, we are interested in summary statistics that can be interpreted as measures of *inequity*. There are a variety of ways to accomplish this when the distribution function to be fit is specified. For example, the exponent in the Pareto distribution is a measure of the inequality of the distribution. However, its interpretation is far from unambiguous.[26] One summary statistic relating to inequality of income or wealth is the so-called Gini coefficient. It has the desirable property that it does not depend on an underlying distribution; that is, it is a "distribution-free" statistic.

The nature of the Gini coefficient or ratio is conveniently explained by reference to the so-called Lorenz curve. This is a plot of the fraction of total social wealth (or income) owned by a given poorest fraction of the

---

25. A large literature surrounds the Pareto "law." See, for example, Kirman [1990] and Persky [1992].

26. See Steindl [1990].

population. Any unequal distribution of wealth produces a Lorenz curve that lies below the 45° line—the poorest X percent of the population controls less than X percent of the society's total wealth. The Gini ratio is a measure of how much the Lorenz curve departs from the 45° line. If everyone has the same amount of wealth the Gini ratio is zero, while if a single individual owns everything then the Gini ratio is one. As the Gini coefficient increases society becomes less egalitarian.[27]

To construct a Lorenz curve for wealth, one first ranks the agents from poorest to wealthiest. Each agent's ranking determines its position along the horizontal axis. Then, for a given agent (abscissa) an ordinate is plotted having a value equal to the total wealth held by the agent and all agents poorer than the agent. The first image in animation II-4 is a Lorenz curve for the initial distribution of wealth on the sugarscape for the run described in animation II-3. When the animation is run, one observes a monotone increase in the curvature of the Lorenz curve—it progressively "bows" outward as inequality grows.

The animation also displays a real-time computation of the Gini coefficient. Note that it starts out quite small (about 0.230) and ends up fairly large (0.503). This Gini ratio, approximately constant for long-time evolutions of the society, is much lower than that seen in industrial societies. In subsequent chapters we shall augment the agents' rules of behavior to include, for example, inheritance, trade, and so on. The Gini ratios of the artificial societies that result then begin to resemble those of developed economies.

The ability to alter agent interaction rules and noiselessly compute the effect on the Gini ratio and other summary statistics is one of the most powerful features of artificial societies. They are "laboratories" for the study of social systems.

Social Networks of Neighbors

As described in Chapter I, we study various agent connection networks in this book. The first of these will be relatively straightforward, adding insight to the basic picture of "hiving" on the sugarscape. Specifically, we want to keep track of each agent's "neighbors."

One might define the term "neighbor" in a variety of ways. Since our

---

27. For a more detailed exposition of the Lorenz curve, see Kakwani [1990]. A concise description of the Gini ratio is Dagum [1990].

Animation II-4. Evolution of the Lorenz Curve and the Gini
Coefficient under Rules ($\{\mathbf{G}_1\}$, $\{\mathbf{M}, \mathbf{R}_{[60,100]}\}$)

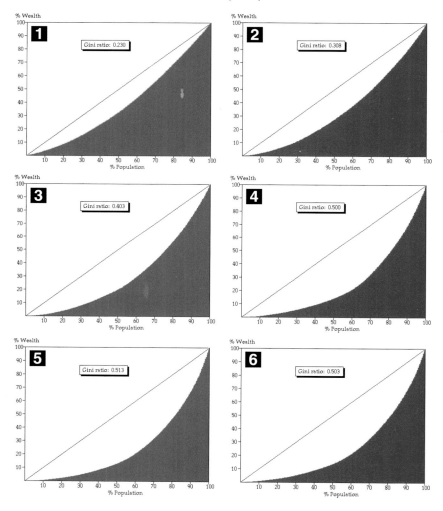

agents live on a rectangular lattice it is natural to use the so-called von
Neumann neighborhood, defined to be the set of sites immediately to
the north, south, east, and west of a particular site. A von Neumann
neighborhood is depicted in figure II-6.

An alternative is the Moore neighborhood, which includes all four
sites of the von Neumann neighborhood as well as the four sites along

Figure II-6. An Agent and Its von Neumann Neighborhood

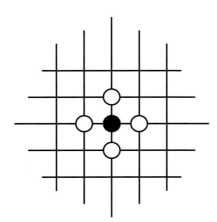

the diagonals. Thus there are eight Moore neighbors as shown in figure II-7.

In what follows we shall always employ the von Neumann neighborhood.[28] When an agent moves to a new position on the sugarscape it has from zero to four neighbors. Each agent keeps track of these neighboring agents internally until it moves again, when it replaces its old neighbors with its new neighbors.

The neighbor connection network is a directed graph with agents as the nodes and edges drawn to the agents who have been their neighbors; it is constructed as follows. Imagine that agents are positioned on the sugarscape and that none has moved. The first agent now executes **M**, moves to a new site, and *then* builds a list of its von Neumann neighbors, which it maintains until its next move. The second agent then moves and builds its list of (post-move) neighbors. The third agent moves and builds its list, and so on until all agents have moved. At this point, lines are drawn from each agent to all agents on its list. The resulting graph—a social network of neighbors—is redrawn after every cycle through the agent population.[29] What is most interesting about such

---

28. In the Sugarscape software system that produced the animations in this book and CD-ROM, one can specify that either a von Neumann or a Moore neighborhood be used.

29. Note that agent-neighbor connections may be asymmetrical (that is, agent i is on agent k's list but not conversely) *and* may extend beyond an agent's von Neumann neighborhood. To see this, imagine that agent i moves into agent k's neighborhood and, accord-

Figure II-7. An Agent and Its Moore Neighborhood

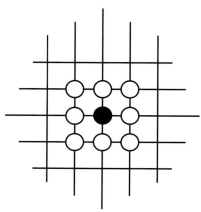

graphs, or networks, is that they change over time as agents (the nodes) move around on the sugarscape. Animation II-5 depicts the development of agent connection networks under rules ($\{\mathbf{G}_1\}$, $\{\mathbf{M}\}$), the same rules that produced animation II-2. Note that some of the neighbor graphs are simple, while others are elaborate webs containing cycles and other structures. Clearly, a rich variety arises.

The connection network reveals something not visible in the earlier animations of agents on the sugarscape. If, for instance, message-passing is permitted only between neighbors, what is the chance that a message could make its way across the entire sugarscape? If we whisper it in the ear of a southwestern agent, will a northeastern one ever hear it? If the world is divided into two spatially separated and noninteracting networks, then neighborwise communication will be limited, and information may be localized in a concrete sense, a phenomenon with important implications in a number of spheres. When agent *interaction* (for example, trade) occurs over such networks, the term "connection network" seems less apt than the term "social network."[30] In essence, the connections describe a topology of social interactions.

---

ingly, puts k on its list. Then, when it's k's turn to move, it hops out of i's neighborhood, so when it builds its (post-move) list, i is not on it. In the resulting graph, then, the edge from i to k will go beyond i's neighborhood, and i will not be on k's list (asymmetry).

30. The literature on social networks is large; Scott [1992] and Kochen [1989] are good introductions. Recent work especially relevant to the dynamic networks presented here

Animation II-5. Evolution of Social Networks of Neighbors under Rules ($\{\mathbf{G}_1\}$, $\{\mathbf{M}\}$)

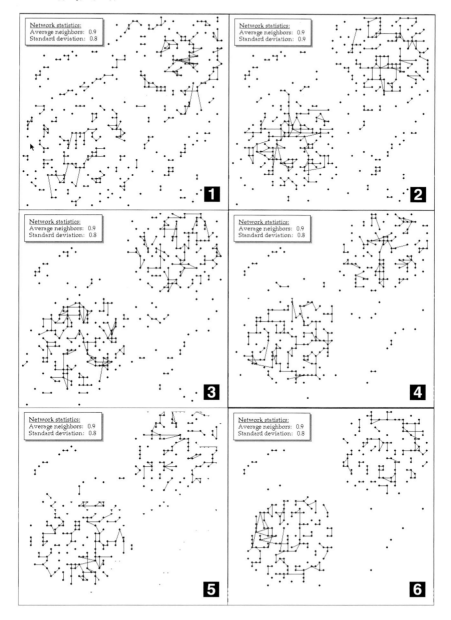

Migration

The skewed wealth distributions above are examples of emergent structures. We turn now to a different kind of emergent structure, this one spatial in nature. To "grow" it we need to give the agents a maximum vision of ten rather than the value of six used above. Now, instead of the random initial distribution of agents on the sugarscape used earlier, suppose they are initially clustered in the dense block shown in the first frame of animation II-6. In all other respects the agents and sugarscape are exactly as in animation II-2. How will this block start affect the dynamics?

A succession of coherent waves results, a phenomenon we did not expect. Reflecting on the local rule, however, the behavior is understandable. Agents in the leading edge proceed to the best unoccupied sugar site within their vision. This leaves a "bald zone" where they had been. The agents behind them must wait until the bald spot grows back under G_1 before they have any incentive, under rule M, to move to those lattice points, and so on for the agents behind them. Hence, the series of waves.[31]

While these waves seem to qualify as emergent structures, the diagonal *direction* in which they propagate is perhaps even more interesting. Recall that during a single application of M the *individual* agent can only move north, south, east, or west. Yet the collective wave is clearly moving northeast—a heading unavailable to individuals! On closer examination, the collective northeast direction results from a complex interweaving of agents, none of whom can move in this direction. This is shown in figure II-8. Here, the local rule *precludes* individual behavior mimicking the collective behavior.[32]

---

includes Banks and Carley [1994a, 1994b], Sanil, Banks, and Carley [1994], and Carley *et al.* [1994].

31. In pure cellular automata (CA) models, waves are phenomena of significant interest. Recently Sato and Iwasa [1993] have produced these in a CA model of forest ecology. Recent attempts by mathematical biologists to model the wavelike movement of certain mammal herds include Gueron and Levin [1993, 1994] and Gueron, Levin, and Rubenstein [1993]. For an economic model of "herding," see Kirman [1993].

32. Thus emergence, in this case, is the opposite of self-similarity, in which a given pattern is observed on all scales (that is, all orders of magnification) as in fractals.

Animation II-6. Emergent Diagonal Waves of Migrators under Rules ({**G**$_1$}, {**M**}) from an Initial Distribution of Agents in a Block

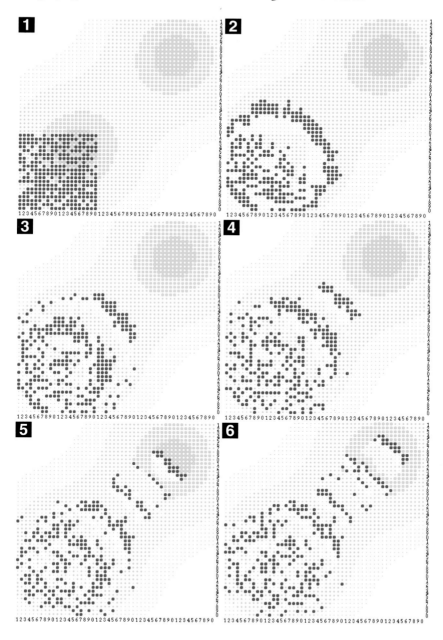

Figure II-8. Interweaving Action of Agents

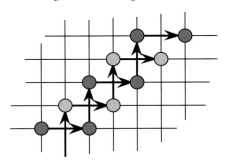

Seasonal Migration

As another example of macrobehavior patterns arising from simple local rules, let us see if our agents can migrate with the seasons. First, to create artificial seasons, we split the familiar sugarscape into a north and a south by drawing an imaginary equator, a horizontal line cutting the sugarscape in half. For the opening season, the sugarscape grows back at unit rate in the north and at one-eighth that rate in the south; it is "bloom" season in the north and "drought" in the south. Then, after fifty time periods, the situation is reversed; the seasons change. The south grows back at unit rate and the north regenerates at one-eighth that rate. And so it goes, season after season. The general rule can be stated as follows:

> Sugarscape seasonal growback rule $\mathbf{S}_{\alpha\beta\gamma}$: Initially it is *summer* in the top half of the sugarscape and *winter* in the bottom half. Then, every γ time periods the seasons flip—in the region where it was summer it becomes winter and vice versa. For each site, if the season is summer then sugar grows back at a rate of α units per time interval; if the season is winter then the growback rate is α units per β time intervals.[33]

---

33. This rule can be stated formally. Noting the time by t, for the sites in the top half (bottom half) of the sugarscape if the value of the quantity

$$\frac{t \bmod (2\gamma)}{\gamma}$$

is less than 1, then the season is summer (winter). Otherwise the season is winter (summer). If the season is summer then the growback rate is α units per time interval. If it is winter it is α units per β time intervals. Here the "mod" operator symbolizes the remainder resulting from an integer division operation; x mod y is the remainder upon division

The question we ask now is this: If the simulation is begun with the same simple agents randomly distributed on the sugarscape, will they migrate back and forth with the seasons? Animation II-7 gives the answer.

Again, the agents, operating under the same simple local rule **M,** exhibit collective behavior far more complex—and far more realistic— than we had expected. Yes, we get migrators. But, we also get "hibernators"! The high vision ("bird-like") creatures migrate. The low vision–low metabolism ("bear-like") creatures hibernate. Agents with low vision and high metabolism generally die; they are selected against.

Notice, however, that a hibernator born in the south rarely goes north, and a hibernator born in the north rarely goes south. Northern and southern hibernators, in short, would rarely meet and, hence, would rarely *mate*. They would form, in effect, separate mating pools and, in evolutionary time, "speciation" would occur.

Pollution: A Negative Externality

So far, in simply grazing the sugarscape, agents have been interacting with one another indirectly. That is, agents move on the basis of what they find in their local environment, and what they find is the result of the actions of other agents.[34] Such indirect interactions are a kind of externality.[35] Externalities can be positive or negative. Pollution is an example of the latter type. A polluter degrades the environment in which other agents live and in so doing reduces the welfare of other agents, and possibly its own welfare as well.

There are many ways in which pollution can be added to the sugarscape. It might be produced by agent movement, agent gathering activities, agent sugar consumption, sugar growback, or some other mechanism. There might be many types of pollutants, each produced at different rates. Pollutants may get transported to other sites at various rates and could possess a natural growth or decay rate. And in order for the pollution to be a negative externality it must affect the agent

---

of x by y. For example, 5 mod 2 = 1. Note that for γ larger than the duration of a run the seasons never change.

34. But the agents do not interact *directly*. In subsequent chapters the agents interact with one another, through behaviors such as sex and trade.

35. When the action of one agent affects the welfare—here, the sugar wealth—of a second agent and is not constrained socially (through a market, for instance), then an externality exists [Campbell, 1987: 57].

Animation II-7. Migration and Hibernation Resulting from Rules ({$\mathbf{S}_{1,8,50}$}, {$\mathbf{M}$}) and a Random Initial Distribution of Agents

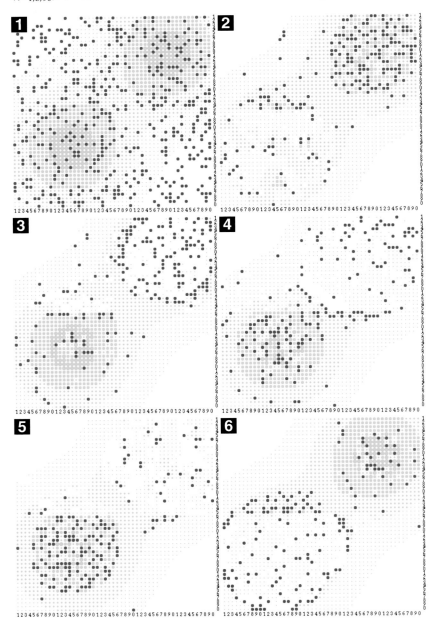

adversely. It could enter the agents' bodies and degrade their vision, say, or increase their metabolisms, as if it made them sick. Or it could simply be a negative amenity—the agents could just dislike it and so try to avoid it whenever possible. In that case it would be as if a second commodity had been added to the sugarscape, an economic "bad."

We have chosen a very simple pollution formation rule. There is one type of pollutant. It is produced by both gathering and consumption activities, in proportion to the amount of sugar gathered and consumed, respectively. It accumulates on the sites at which the gathering and consumption activities occur. Stated formally, the rule is:

Pollution formation rule $P_{\alpha\beta}$: When sugar quantity s is gathered from the sugarscape, an amount of production pollution is generated in quantity αs. When sugar amount m is consumed (metabolized), consumption pollution is generated according to βm. The total pollution on a site at time t, p^t, is the sum of the pollution present at the previous time, plus the pollution resulting from production and consumption activities, that is, $p^t = p^{t-1} + \alpha s + \beta m$.[36]

Pollution affects the agents in a very simple way: it has negative amenity value. That is, they just do not like it! The simplest way to incorporate this is to modify the agent movement rule somewhat, to let the pollution devalue—in the agents' eyes—the sites where it is present. Instead of moving to the site of maximum sugar, we now specify that the agents select the site having the maximum sugar to pollution ratio.[37] That is, those sites with high sugar levels and low pollution levels are the most attractive. The modified agent movement rule now reads (with the changes to the previous rule italicized):

Agent movement rule **M**, modified for pollution:
- Look out as far as vision permits in the four principal lattice directions and identify the unoccupied site(s) having the maximum *sugar to pollution ratio*;

---

36. The Sugarscape software system offers a more general pollution formation rule than this. There can be multiple types of pollutants, each produced at different rates. In Chapter IV, when investigating the effect of pollution on prices and economic trade activity, we shall make use of the general pollution formation rule. This more general rule is described fully in Appendix B, along with the general forms of all other rules.

37. To be precise, the ratio computed is actually $s/(1+p)$ to preclude division by zero in the no pollution case.

- If the maximum *sugar to pollution ratio* appears on multiple sites, then select the nearest one;
- Move to this site;
- Collect all the sugar at this new position.

The final ingredient to add is some form of pollution transport. Without transport or dissipation pollution simply accumulates without bound at the sites where it is produced. Perhaps the simplest form of transport is diffusion. Diffusion on a lattice like the sugarscape is simply implemented as a local averaging procedure. That is, diffusion transports pollution from sites of high levels to sites of low levels. This can be stated algorithmically as:

Pollution diffusion rule $\mathbf{D}_\alpha$:
- Each α time periods and at each site, compute the pollution flux—the average pollution level over all von Neumann neighboring sites;
- Each site's flux becomes its new pollution level.

The reader with a knowledge of cellular automata (CA) will notice that this rule, which relates the pollution on any site to that on other sites, makes the sugarscape a true CA.[38] Note that as α is increased the rate of diffusion is decreased, so $\mathbf{D}_1$ is the fastest diffusion possible.

These simple rules, taken together, prove sufficient to "grow" a reasonable story of agent response to an agent polluted environment. In animation II-8 agents execute the modified movement rule, $\mathbf{M}$. The sugarscape grows back according to $\mathbf{G}_1$. At $t = 50$ pollution begins (rule $\mathbf{P}_{11}$ is turned on). Then, at $t = 100$, diffusion begins (rule $\mathbf{D}_1$ is switched on).

At first the agents are merrily hiving the sugar hills, as usual. Pollution levels are low, and the behavior produced by the modified movement rule is not much different from that produced by the original movement rule. Eventually, however, pollution levels build up and the agents progressively abandon the polluted zone. They are forced off the sugar

38. The simple growback rule $\mathbf{G}_\alpha$ does this only trivially since growback rates on any site are independent of either growback rates or sugar levels on neighboring sites. We have experimented with growback rules that do, in fact, have this dependence. One such rule is as follows: if the level of sugar is not 0, then apply $\mathbf{G}_\alpha$; however, if the sugar level is 0, then grow back only if some neighboring site has a nonzero sugar level. It is as if each barren site must be "seeded" by neighbors.

Animation II-8. Agent Migration in a Polluted Environment; Rule System ($\{\mathbf{G}_1, \mathbf{D}_1\}, \{\mathbf{M}, \mathbf{P}_{11}\}$)

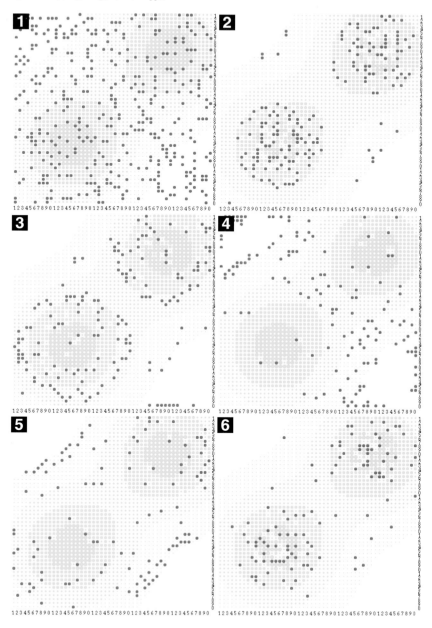

peaks, migrating into relatively pristine areas where no pollution from sugar production has accumulated. However, as agents continue to eat from their personal accumulations, they progressively despoil even this area through consumption pollution. Because there is little food for the agents out in this resource-poor hinterland, competition is intense. Many die of starvation—the carrying capacity of the polluted environment is lower.

Subsequently, when diffusion is turned on, the pollution quickly spreads more or less uniformly around the landscape and many agents move back to the regions of highest sugar. As they continue to gather and metabolize sugar, pollution increases while diffusing over the entire landscape. There is a kind of rising "red tide" that diminishes the welfare of all agents still alive on the sugarscape.[39]

It turns out that the same type of dynamic pattern appears when the externality involved is positive rather than negative. Positive externalities—increasing returns or network externalities, for example—give agents reasons to associate with one another, to spatially cluster. Of course, the two types of externalities can be combined: there may be positive externalities associated with production but negative externalities associated with consumption. Are cities the "balance points" between these opposed effects?[40]

A Social Interpretation

It is possible to give a social intrepretation to the migratory dynamics just discussed. When seasons change or pollution levels rise, large numbers of agents migrate to particular regions of the sugarscape. In effect, they

---

39. It is at this point that a clear "tragedy of the commons" interpretation of life on the sugarscape manifests itself. Metabolisms are constant and so, for a fixed agent population, sugar consumption and the pollution it generates are fixed; thus, the only way pollution levels can be decreased is to reduce the amount of pollution generated through production (harvesting) activities. If, for instance, those agents who harvest more sugar than they consume in following **M** were to follow some alternative rule, harvesting only, say, half the sugar they find beyond their metabolic needs, then overall pollution levels would fall. While this behavioral rule would make these agents worse off, in comparison to **M**, by lowering their income, perhaps all agents could be made better off through side payments. Alternative rules—institutions—for managing such common property resource problems in general are investigated at length by Ostrom [1990] and Ostrom, Gardner, and Walker [1994].

40. For a very general analysis along these lines, see Papageorgiou and Smith [1993]; see also Krugman [1996].

are environmental refugees; an environmental catastrophe has struck their zone and they flood into better areas. In Chapter III, we introduce combat. Its intensity can grow when competition for resources becomes severe. An influx of environmental refugees suddenly boosts the agent density in the receiving zone and, naturally, competition for sugar intensifies dramatically. The model suggests, therefore, that *environmental degradation can have serious security implications.*[41]

Summary

These exercises make clear that a wide range of collective structures and collective patterns of behavior can emerge from the spatio-temporal interaction of agents operating, individually, under simple local rules. For example, only one agent rule, **M**, has been used, and it is about as primitive a rule as we could construct. Paraphrasing, it amounts to the instruction: "Look around for the best free site; go there and harvest the sugar." And yet, all sorts of unexpected things emerge from the *interaction* of these agents: basic principles like the existence of environmental carrying capacities; skewed distributions of wealth; coherent group structures like waves that move in directions unavailable to individuals; and biological processes like hibernation and migration (refugees). And that strikes us as surprising. The nature of the surprise is worth discussing.

The Surprising Sufficiency of Simple Rules

We have succeeded in "growing" a number of quite familiar collective behaviors, such as migration, and familiar macroscopic structures, such as skewed wealth distributions. And we grow many more familiar macroscopic entities below. Now, upon first exposure to these familiar social, or macroscopic, structures—be they migrations, skewed wealth distributions, or the like—some people say, "Yes, that looks familiar. But, I've seen it before. What's the surprise?"

The surprise consists precisely in the emergence of familiar macrostructures *from the bottom up*—from simple local rules that out-

---

41. The connection between environmental change and security is the subject of several recent studies by Homer-Dixon [1991, 1994]. The mathematical structure of spatial patterns resulting from conflicts has been studied by Vickers, Hutson, and Budd [1993].

wardly appear quite remote from the social, or collective, phenomena they generate. In short, *it is not the emergent macroscopic object per se that is surprising, but the generative sufficiency of the simple local rules.*

Of course, for the model to be of practical use to social scientists, a minimum requirement is that it generate familiar phenomena with some fidelity. If the model cannot generate the familiar world as a base case, then how can we use it to examine the effects of various policies, for example?

Furthermore, there may be familiar and important social phenomena that are hard to study with standard tools. For instance, we can do more than turn pollution on and off in our model; we can track its effect on prices (see Chapter IV). We find that a pollution-induced shortage of one good increases its price, an effect described in standard economics texts. But when we then diffuse the pollutant, relieving the shortage, relative prices do not return to equilibrium instantly—on the contrary, the adjustment may take a long time. And adjustment *dynamics* are difficult to model within the standard equilibrium framework. Moreover, had we been unable to get the familiar result (that is, the "right" price response to shortage), this lag in adjustment would not be credible.

The main point, however, is that, when—in subsequent chapters—we grow a familiar macrostructure, it is the sufficiency of the local rules that is surprising.

Artificial Social Systems as Laboratories

Of course, in this exposition, we presented the rules *before* carrying out any simulations. We might have proceeded differently. Imagine that we had begun the entire discussion by simply running animation II-2, which shows a buzz of agents "hiving" the sugar mountains, and that we had then bluntly asked, "What's happening here?" Would you have guessed that the agents are all following rule **M**? We do not think we would have been able to divine it. But that really is all that is happening. Isn't it just possible that something comparably simple is "all that is happening" in other complex systems, such as stock markets or political systems? As social scientists, this is the problem we normally confront. We observe the complex collective—already emerged—behavior, and we seek simple local rules of individual behavior (for example, maximize profit) that could generate it.

The Sugarscape model can function as a kind of *laboratory* where we "grow" fundamental social structures *in silico*, thereby learning which micromechanisms are sufficient to generate macrostructures of interest. Such experiments can lead to hypotheses of social concern that may subsequently be tested statistically against data.

In Chapter III we expand the behavioral repertoire of our agents, allowing us to study more complex social phenomena.

Sex, Culture, and Conflict:
The Emergence of History

The basic aim of this chapter is to "grow" a very simple caricature of history—a "proto-history," if you will. History unfolds on the "twin-peaked" sugarscape familiar from Chapter II, with the sugarscape following the unit growback rule, G_1. The agents once again move according to rule **M** but now have other behavioral modes as well, including sex, cultural exchange, and combat. The social story is as follows:

> *In the beginning, there is a small population of agents, randomly distributed both in space and with respect to their genetic characteristics. Over time spatial agglomeration into two groups occurs as each agent—guided by the primal sugar drive—migrates to one of the two sugar peaks. There, in the midst of plenty, the pioneer agents interact sexually, producing children, who in turn beget children, and so on. All the while processes of cultural evolution are operating within each group producing culturally distinct "tribes" of agents on the two mountains. Ultimately, as population pressures mount from overexploitation of the sugar resources, each tribe spreads down into the central sugar lowlands between the two mountains. When the two tribes ultimately collide, processes of assimilation occur and feed back on the reproductive and cultural activities of the tribes, yielding complex social evolutions.*

Our goal, as always, is to grow this history "from the bottom up." Can the entire social history—along with all sorts of variants—be made to emerge from the interaction of agents operating under simple local rules?[1]

In what follows we consider matters of sex first, followed by cultural transmission and the formation of groups, then combat between indi-

---

1. Since it is not a quantitatively exact story, the "proto-history" admits many realizations. The issue is whether we can grow one of these with the ingredients developed in this chapter.

viduals belonging to different groups, concluding with the promised "proto-history."

Sexual Reproduction

Can we develop an agent-based demography in which the main dynamics observed in populations *emerge* from the local interactions of the individuals? Minimally, we would like to be able to "grow" the full range of observed aggregate population trajectories, including relatively stable population levels and large oscillations. Variables like "fertility rate," which are treated as exogenous, often fixed, coefficients in many standard "top-down" demographic models, are in fact highly heterogeneous and should emerge as a result of agent-agent and agent-environment couplings. When fertility rates and population densities begin to interact on the sugarscape, we in fact find that extinction events—central topics of paleontology and evolutionary biology generally—can arise endogenously, without the aid of meteor impacts or other outside agencies. Finally, we expect natural selection to be observable over long times, which indeed it is in Sugarscape.

Imagine that some agent has just arrived at a new sugarscape location as a result of following some movement rule, for example, **M**. After moving, agents are permitted to engage in sexual reproduction with their neighbors. But they must be fertile.

Fertility

First, to have offspring, agents must be of childbearing age. Second, children born with literally no initial endowment of sugar would instantly die. We therefore require that parents give their children some initial endowment. Each newborn's endowment is the sum of the (usually unequal) contributions of mother and father. Dad contributes an amount equal to one half of whatever his initial endowment had been, and likewise for mom.[2] To be parents, agents must have amassed at least the amount of sugar with which they were endowed at birth. (In Chapter IV we will permit agents to borrow from other agents to meet this need.) Agents meeting these age and wealth requirements are

---

2. Agents of the very first generation are assigned random initial endowments.

defined as "fertile." Each fertile agent executes sex rule **S**, which may be stated algorithmically as follows:

Agent sex rule **S**:
- Select a neighboring agent at random;
- If the neighbor is fertile *and* of the opposite sex *and* at least one of the agents has an empty neighboring site (for the baby), then a child is born;
- Repeat for all neighbors.

It might be that the agent has four neighbors and each is a viable partner. In that case the agent mates with each of them before it is the next agent's turn to move.[3] (However, this possibility is realized infrequently in that agents, if fertile, rarely possess enough wealth to have multiple children in a single period.)

From birth, the baby agent follows **M** just as mature agents do—looking around, accumulating sugar, and so on. The sex of each child is random—males and females are equally likely. The child's genetic makeup (metabolism, vision, maximum age, and so forth) is determined from parental genetics through Mendelian rules. As the simplest illustration, consider only metabolism and vision and imagine one parent to be of type (m, v) while the other parent is genetically (M, V). Then there are four equally likely genotypes for their child: (m, v), (m, V), (M, v), and (M, V), the combinations given in table III-1.

The agents produced by sexual reproduction are genetically *heterogeneous*. They are *heterogeneous,* too, from the perspective of their environmental attributes; for example, their positions and sugar accumulations. They are *homogeneous* with regard to their behavioral rules, since they all execute {**M**, **S**}. But their *behavior*—as distinct from their *behavioral rules*—is *heterogeneous* since each agent has somewhat different opportunities (depending on which part of the sugarscape it occupies) as well as different abilities (since genetic attributes are parameters of behavioral rules).

Now all of this may seem a cumbersome apparatus. But it is the simplest one we could devise. In fact, it turns out that this set of *local* repro-

---

3. After observing that the sex rule **S** occasionally yielded multiple births per time period—an outcome we had not considered before running the model—we were tempted to augment the rule with additional conditions such as "females can have only one baby per time period." However, given our wish to keep the rules as simple as possible, we decided not to add more conditions. Similarly, we have not prohibited sexual relations between close relatives.

Table III-1. Crossover of Genetic Attributes in Sexual Reproduction

Vision	Metabolism	
	m	M
v	(m, v)	(M, v)
V	(m, V)	(M, V)

ductive rules and regulations—the sex code—gives rise to a rich variety of *global*, or macroscopic, population dynamics.

To study demography on the sugarscape it is not particularly revealing to look down on the agents as they gather sugar and reproduce sexually. Rather, a time series of the total number of agents succinctly summarizes the overall dynamics. We present several time series of this type below for various parameterizations of the rule **S**.

Calling each time period of the model a "year," we first study a population of agents having the following characteristics:[4]

- for both men and women, childbearing begins between the ages of 12 and 15;
- for women, childbearing terminates between the ages of 40 and 50;
- for men, childbearing terminates between the ages of 50 and 60;
- for both men and women, the age of natural death is between 60 and 100;
- members of the initial population have initial endowments in the range 50 to 100 sugar units.

Combining all of this with the movement rule **M** and the sugarscape growback rule **G**$_1$, population dynamics result. A typical aggregate population time series is shown in figure III-1.

Note that the total number of agents is more or less constant. There seem to be some small quasi-oscillations but these have magnitude less than 10 percent of the overall population level.

While the population is essentially constant in this case it is important to remember that many distinct generations of agents make up figure III-1. That is, the constancy of the total population is actually the result of an approximately *stationary age distribution* of agents. In the artificial society of Sugarscape we can study this distribution directly. Animation

---

4. For any particular agent the actual value of a parameter is a random variable in the stated range.

Figure III-1. Time Series of Aggregate Population under Rules ({**G**₁}, {**M**, **S**})

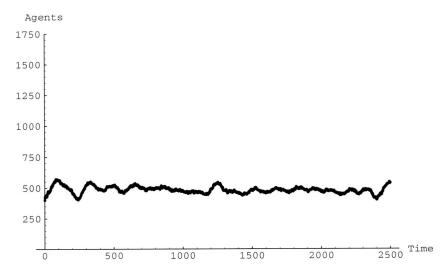

III-1 is the age distribution corresponding to figure III-1, changing over time.

Along the horiziontal axis of the figure are age cohort bins, while the vertical axis gives the number of agents falling into each bin. Age distributions highly skewed to the left represent young societies in which there is a high rate of childbirth, while those highly skewed to the right represent aging societies. This age distribution, as mentioned above, assumes an approximately stationary configuration.

Although the total number of agents is approximately constant in this case, it is not true that the characteristics of the agents are unchanging. We explore this presently.

The Theory of Evolution Brought to Life

Agents with relatively low metabolism and high vision enjoy a selective advantage on the sugarscape. Indeed, one can actually watch evolution in action here by coloring agents according to their genetic attributes. First, we color the agents according to their vision. At the start of the run there is a uniform distribution of vision from 1 to 6 among the agents. We color an agent blue if it has vision 1, 2, or 3 and red if it has vision 4, 5, or 6.

Animation III-1. Age Histogram Evolution under Rules ($\{\mathbf{G}_1\}$, $\{\mathbf{M}, \mathbf{S}\}$)

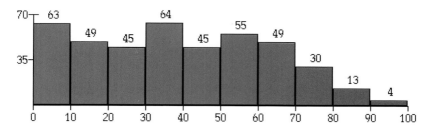

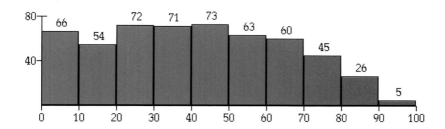

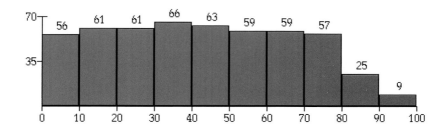

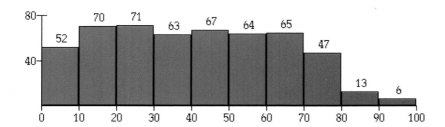

Animation III-2. Societal Evolution under Rules ($\{G_1\}$, $\{M, S\}$), Coloring by Agent Vision

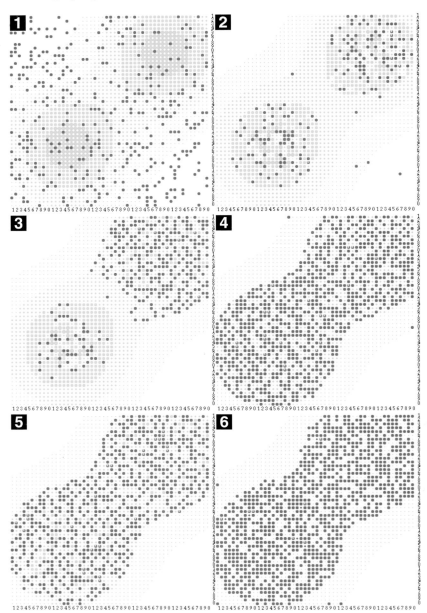

Watch animation III-2 and note how the colors of the agents change.

At first there are nearly equal numbers of red and blue agents, but over time there is a trend toward more red (high vision) agents. Evolution happens here because of the fertility advantage high vision bestows on agents who have it—high vision yields more sugar income, which begets more children.[5]

Next we do the same thing for metabolism; agents are colored blue if their metabolism is below the initial population mean, red if it is above. Metabolism for sugar is initially uniformly distributed among the agents in the range 1 to 4. But over time evolution eats away at the high metabolism elements of the population, producing, in the end, agents having a uniformly low metabolism. The reader can watch this in animation III-3.

These genetic characteristics—vision and metabolism—affect the ability of agents to survive on the sugarscape in an unambiguous way; *ceteris paribus,* high vision out-gathers low vision and high metabolism makes survival more difficult. Thus the direction in which the mean values of these characteristics move evolutionarily is intuitively clear.[6] A time series plot of the mean vision and metabolism from animations III-2 and III-3 is given in figure III-2.

This plot makes clear the speed and power of evolutionary processes on the sugarscape. Interestingly, the average metabolism falls faster than the average vision rises. Moreover, the increase in vision—evolutionary "progress"—is not strictly monotone; there are short periods during which the mean actually decreases!

Our population of agents (each of whom possesses its bundle of genetic attributes) can be fruitfully thought of as evolving according to a kind of genetic algorithm. This is so because our sex rule, **S**, involves crossover of the parents' genetic attributes. However, we have nowhere explicitly defined a fitness function. Rather, we have merely stated rules of reproduction and, from this, endogenous fitness emerges (locally) on the sugarscape. It emerges from agent-environment and agent-agent interactions.[7]

In fact, it is not clear that "fitness" abstracted from all environmental

---

5. Notice that evolution occurs even though we have *not* defined an exogenous fitness function. We will return to this point.

6. In Chapter IV we will introduce another genetic parameter that has a more ambiguous effect on the ability of agents to survive—a foresight parameter—and we will study its complicated evolution there.

7. On endogenous or intrinsic fitness, see Packard [1989] and Langton [1989: 38].

Animation III-3. Societal Evolution under Rules ({G_1}, {**M**, **S**}), Coloring by Agent Metabolism

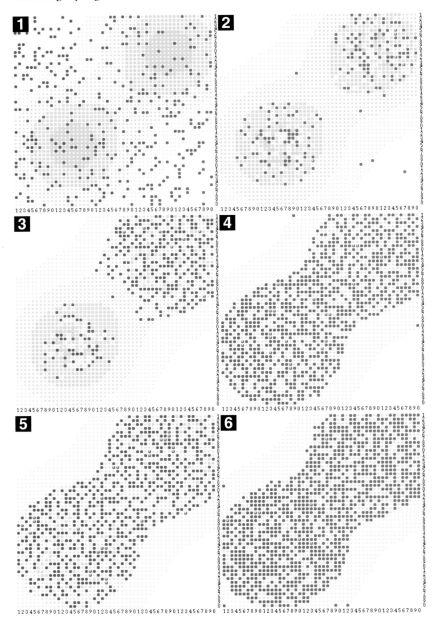

Figure III-2. Evolution of Mean Agent Vision and Metabolism under Rules ($\{G_1\}, \{M, S\}$)

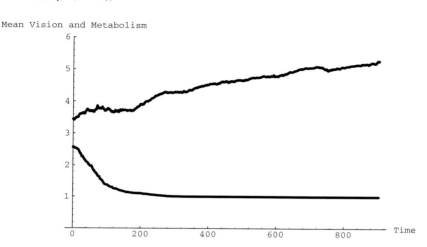

Mean Vision and Metabolism

conditions can be usefully defined. To illustrate this point, suppose we—as gods of Sugarscape—simply set the agents' vision to some high level, boosting their foraging efficiency and, through **S**, their reproductive rates. On one reading, the average fitness in society would appear to be higher than before. But suppose these "fitter" agents bring on their own extinction—through a combination of overgrazing and explosive reproduction! Then it obviously was not so "fit" after all for everybody to have exceedingly high vision.[8] *Sustainable coevolution with one's environment* is a necessary condition for "fitness," if we wish to retain this term at all.[9] Sugarscape invites us to conceive of fitness as another emergent property, not as something—such as vision—that can be determined by inspection of individuals in isolation.

Our concerns in this section have been with the genetic composition of the population. What of population levels? This is of course a crucial issue for policy and a major ingredient of the "proto-history." What

---

8. Ackley and Littman [1992] perform a related experiment in their artificial ecology.
9. On conceptual difficulties surrounding the notion of fitness and related issues, see Sober [1994] and Cohen [1985].

Figure III-3. Small Amplitude Population Oscillations under Rules ({**G**$_1$}, {**M**, **S**})

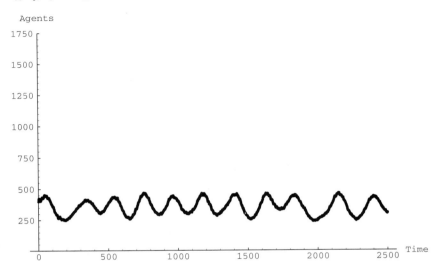

determines population growth and how does it interact with other variables, such as fertility? We now return to population dynamics proper.

Regimes of Population Dynamics

More interesting than the constant population level of figure III-1 and the corresponding stationary age distribution shown in animation III-1 are situations in which birth rates and population size may vary periodically. This leads to a distribution of ages oscillating between two limiting distributions. It turns out that such an outcome can be produced by employing sex rule **S** with a single change to the parameters: For both men and women, fertility terminates 10 years earlier than before; that is,

- for women, childbearing terminates between the ages of 30 and 40;
- for men, childbearing terminates between the ages of 40 and 50.

In this case the sex rule produces the time series given in figure III-3.

Note the fairly regular oscillations. These are bounded in amplitude, and the population never falls below about 250. The period of the oscillations appears to be around 200 years. Perhaps the most interesting feature of this cyclic aggregate behavior is that it is produced completely "from the bottom up"—through the individual actions and interactions

Figure III-4. Large Amplitude Population Oscillations under Rules
($\{\mathbf{G}_1\}$, $\{\mathbf{M}, \mathbf{S}\}$)

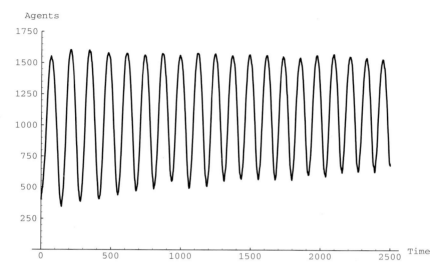

of myriad agents.[10] Furthermore, given that the average agent's lifetime
is approximately 80 years, the 200-year period of the oscillation means
that no single agent ever participates in an entire population swing.

There are other ways to produce population oscillations on the sugarscape. If we restore the previous limits on the ages at which infertility
sets in but reduce the amount of sugar necessary for reproduction to the
range 10 to 40, we get the population trajectory depicted in figure III-4.

Now the amplitude of oscillation starts out at over 1000, gradually
diminishing to approximately 800. The frequency of these oscillations is
approximately 125 years. Compared with the previous oscillations these
are much more energetic.

Finally, when the variations in **S** that produced figures III-3 and III-4
are combined—decreased duration of fertility and decreased wealth
requirements—the population may oscillate so severely that, at some
point, a minimum population occurs that has too little diversity or is spatially too thin (that is, permits too little mating) to re-initiate a cycle of
growth. Such an outcome is shown in figure III-5, where the society suf-
fers extinction after completing three growth surges.

---

10. Over the 2500 time periods represented in figure III-3, some 12,500 agents inhabit the sugarscape.

Figure III-5. Severe Population Swings Leading to Extinction under Rules ($\{\mathbf{G}_1\}$, $\{\mathbf{M}, \mathbf{S}\}$)

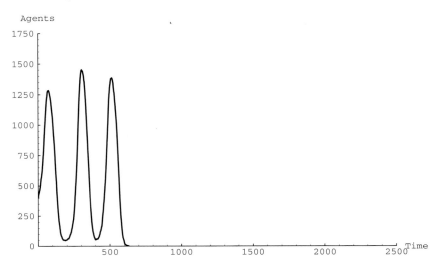

In many fields there are ongoing debates concerning the role of endogenous (internally generated) versus exogenous (externally imposed) factors in explaining important phenomena. In paleontology and related fields there are longstanding exogenous-endogenous debates about extinction events. Do they require external shocks, or can the internal dynamics of the system itself bring them about?[11] Our agent-based modeling suggests that internal dynamics alone are *sufficient to generate* cataclysmic events.

We summarize the various regimes of population dynamics described above in figure III-6.

Clearly, a great variety of macroscopic dynamics can be produced by this simple model. In subsequent chapters we will study ways in which population dynamics are coupled to other social processes.

Nature and Nurture: The Genetic Effect of Inheritance

What is the relationship of social institutions—such as property rights—to processes of biological evolution? This is the type of interdisciplinary question that traditional fields do not normally address. Biology does not

---

11. Recently Hastings and Higgins [1994] have obtained very complex population dynamics in a spatially distributed ecological model.

Figure III-6. Regimes of Population Dynamics under Rules
($\{\mathbf{G}_1\}, \{\mathbf{M}, \mathbf{S}\}$) for Various Parameters

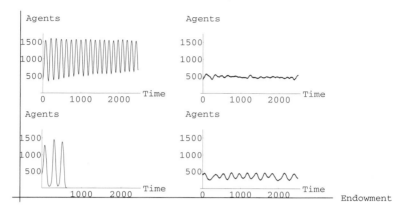

include economics and vice versa. But in an artificial society we can
study biology and economics at once.

In the runs described above, when an agent dies all its wealth simply
disappears. We saw evolution at work and watched as average metabolism fell and average vision rose over time. Now let us allow agents to
pass their accumulated holdings of sugar on to their offspring when they
die; that is, we permit inheritance. Formally, this involves defining a
new rule of agent-agent (parent-child) interaction.

> Agent inheritance rule **I**: When an agent dies its wealth is equal-
> ly divided among all its living children.[12]

How does this *social* convention affect *biological* evolution—in particular,
what happens to the trajectories of average metabolism and average
vision over time? We have rerun the model under exactly the conditions
that produced figure III-2, only now letting rule **I** be active. Time series
for average vision and metabolism have been overlaid in red on those of
figure III-2 in figure III-7.

In the case of vision the message is clear: *Inheritance retards selection.*
Agents who might otherwise have been "weeded out" are given an

---

12. In the Sugarscape software system, other inheritance schemes may be selected by
the user, including division of wealth among sons, daughters, or friends.

Figure III-7. Evolution of Mean Agent Vision and Metabolism under Rules ($\{G_1\}$, $\{M, S, I\}$)

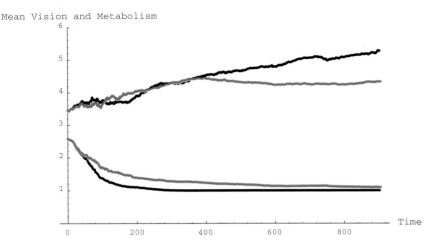

advantage through inheritance. However, it does not seem that inheritance has a comparable effect on metabolism, given how the two (lower) curves for this genetic attribute ultimately meet.

Interestingly, some "Social Darwinists" oppose wealth transfers *to the poor* on the ground that the undiluted operation of selective pressures is "best for the species." Conveniently, they fail to mention that intergenerational transfers of wealth *from the rich to their offspring* dilute those very pressures.

Inheritance raises the Gini coefficient in society—inequality grows under inheritance. This is shown in animation III-4.

In the previous chapter we noted that the Gini ratio produced by the rule system ($\{G_1\}$, $\{M, R_{[60,100]}\}$) was small in comparison to that of real economies. With inheritance the Gini ratio is far higher, reaching as high as 0.743 here.[13]

Genealogical Networks

In Chapter II a neighborhood network was defined. Here the sex rule provides a natural basis for a well-known social network, the "family

---

13. Brittain [1977, 1978] analyzes inheritance data for the United States.

Animation III-4. Evolution of the Lorenz Curve and Gini Coefficient
under Rules ({$\mathbf{G_1}$}, {$\mathbf{M}$, $\mathbf{S}$, $\mathbf{I}$})

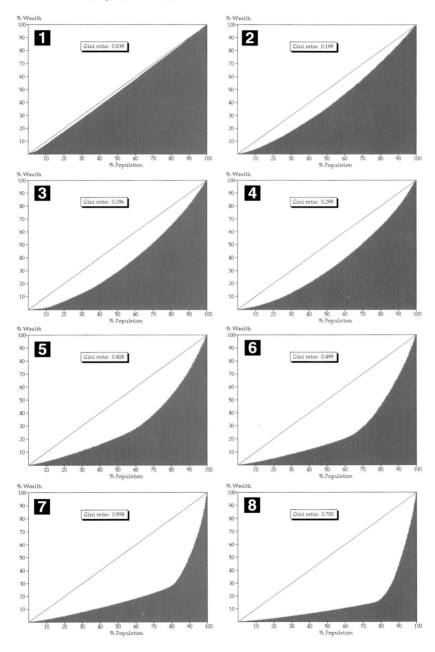

Animation III-5. Evolution of Genealogical Networks under Rules ($\{\mathbf{G}_1\}$, $\{\mathbf{M}, \mathbf{S}\}$)

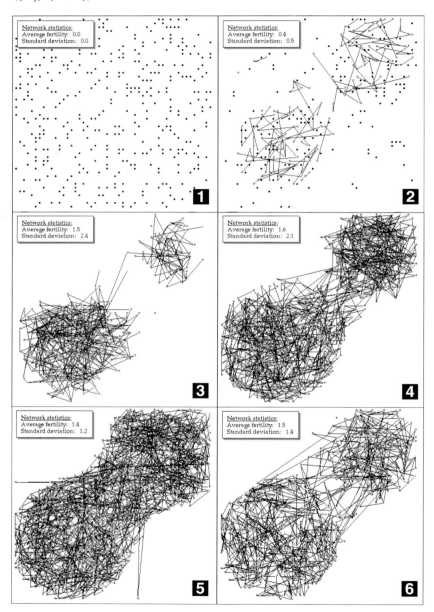

Network statistics:
Average fertility: 0.0
Standard deviation: 0.0

Network statistics:
Average fertility: 0.4
Standard deviation: 0.5

Network statistics:
Average fertility: 1.5
Standard deviation: 2.4

Network statistics:
Average fertility: 1.6
Standard deviation: 2.1

Network statistics:
Average fertility: 1.4
Standard deviation: 1.2

Network statistics:
Average fertility: 1.5
Standard deviation: 1.4

tree." This is depicted in animation III-5 by drawing a line from every parent to each of its children.[14] The initial population is colored black. When a member of this population has a child, the new parent is colored red, the child green. Agents who are both parents and children are colored yellow. (Note that members of the initial population can never be yellow.)

It is interesting to watch the evolution of such genealogical networks. At the outset there are no connections since, in the initial population, no agents are related. However, after several generations, when none of the initial agents remains, all the agents on the sugarscape have some definite genealogical lineage. Notice that average fertility and the standard deviation in fertility both vary substantially in the course of this run.

We have made an initial foray into agent-based demography. The range of phenomena obtained is heartening. Clearly, this is a rich area and our efforts barely scratch the surface. With this first ingredient of the proto-history—sexual reproduction and endogenous population dynamics—in hand, we now proceed to the second, the formation of cultural groups.

Cultural Processes

Our simple agents may not yet seem quite human since all they do is move, eat, and procreate. In this section we give our agents internal states representing cultural factors and augment their behavioral repertoire with simple local rules for cultural interchange. This proves sufficient to produce agent populations having dynamic, heterogeneous cultures. Then, given that any two agents may be either similar or different culturally, it makes sense to talk about distinct cultural formations or tribes of agents. Indeed, we will "grow" such tribes here "from the bottom up."[15]

---

14. This is implemented by, among other things, having each agent keep pointers to all of its children.

15. Axelrod [1995] studies a bottom-up model of culture in which the agents maintain fixed positions on a two-dimensional lattice. Axtell *et al.* [1996] discuss an implementation of Axelrod's culture model in Sugarscape and the usefulness of such "docking" experiments for agent-based social science.

Cultural Tags

Recall that every agent is born with a genetic endowment: a metabolism, a vision, a sex, and so forth. Although the distribution of these genetic attributes changes from generation to generation, the genetic makeup of any particular agent is fixed over its lifetime. Of course, in reality, important attributes (for example, tastes) *do* change in the course of one's life.[16] We wish to capture processes of this sort. So beyond its fixed genetic endowment, each agent is born with a structure that represents its cultural attributes. This is a string of zeros and ones.[17] The length of this nongenetic string is the same for all agents.[18] For example, an agent might have a cultural string consisting of 10011010011. We will refer to each element of the string as a tag and will often call the entire structure a "tag string," or simply the agent's "tags." Agents can change one another's tags, which causes the distribution of tags in society to change over time.

Cultural Transmission

Consider an agent who has just landed at some site on the sugarscape. That agent—let us call her Rose—has up to four von Neumann neighbors (as discussed in Chapter II). For illustration, imagine she has two; call them A and B. Cultural transmission might proceed in a great variety of ways. We will adopt the following tag-flipping scheme. First, a neighbor is selected, say neighbor A. Then, one of Rose's tag positions is selected at random. Suppose it is position six and suppose Rose has a 1 at that position—a cultural tag of 1. Then, if neighbor A has a tag of 0 at that position (its position six), it gets flipped to Rose's value of 1. If, at that position, neighbor A already matches Rose, no flip occurs. Now Rose moves on to neighbor B. Again, one of Rose's tag positions is

---

16. In fact, there is a longstanding debate in economics as to whether or not preferences for commodities change during one's life. This is a topic to which we will return in Chapter IV, where we use the cultural exchange apparatus described here to model preferences that vary.

17. The idea that cultural attributes might be profitably modeled as if they were alleles on a cultural chromosome—called "memes" by Dawkins [1976: 206]—has been studied systematically by Cavalli-Sforza and Feldman [1981] and applied to problems of gene-culture coevolution, such as the lactose absorption problem [Feldman and Cavalli-Sforza, 1989]. Related work includes Boyd and Richerson [1985].

18. In the Sugarscape software system, the string length is a user-specified parameter. We have experimented with lengths from 1 to 1000.

selected at random. If, at that position, neighbor B already matches Rose, no change is made. Otherwise, neighbor B's tag is flipped to agree with Rose's tag at that position. Rose's turn is then over, and it is the next agent's turn to flip its neighbor's tags. A summary statement follows.

Cultural transmission rule (tag-flipping):
- For each neighbor, a tag is randomly selected;
- If the neighbor agrees with the agent at that tag position, no change is made; if they disagree, the neighbor's tag is flipped to agree with the agent's tag.[19]

Now, imagine that we start with a primordial soup of agents with random genetics, random tag strings, and random initial positions on the sugarscape. In the course of an agent's life, its movement, based on the sugar drive, brings it into the neighborhoods of all sorts of other agents, who may flip its tags, just as we, in the course of our lives, may be influenced—in our tastes or beliefs—by contact with other individuals.

Cultural Groups

Having fixed on a tag transformation rule, a separate issue is how to define groups. As usual, we choose to do it in a simple fashion.

Group membership rule (tag majority): Agents are defined to be members of the Blue group when 0s outnumber 1s on their tag strings, and members of the Red group in the opposite case.[20]

---

19. Many other cultural transmission rules are possible. An agent might flip n of its neighbors' tags, not just one, as above. Or, reversing roles, it could be neighbors who flip the agent's tags, k at a time. Or, agents and neighbors could *swap* tags, and so on. Eigen and Winkler [1981] have considered a variety of rules in the guise of "statistical bead games."

20. Many other rules for group membership are possible. One might identify particular positions—or sequences thereof—with certain groups. Tag position five might encode an agent's religion (0 for Muslim, 1 for Catholic). Group membership could require tag unanimity, with one tribe having all 0s and the other having all 1s. For tag strings of length 11, one three-group scheme is given below.

Agent Group	Number of Zeros on String
Blue	0 – 3
Green	4 – 7
Red	8 – 11

By increasing the string length and introducing considerations of tag ordering, very refined schemes become possible.

So, an agent with tag string 01010001010 would be a Blue, while one with 01001110101 a Red.[21] Since tag order is irrelevant here we might call this a "voting rule."

Notation

We have been denoting all rules with bold-faced letters (for example, **M** for movement). In principle, we could allot separate symbols for our cultural transmission (tag-flipping) and group membership (tag majority) rules. But, since we will only employ these rules together, we collapse them into a single symbol, **K**, which denotes this combination.

Cultural Dynamics

Recall that one component of the "proto-history" is the formation of spatially segregated, culturally distinct groups. Are the simple rules elaborated above *sufficient to generate* such outcomes? Returning to the familiar sugarscape, let us begin with a population of agents with random genetics, random tag strings each of length eleven, and random initial locations. The sugarscape grows back at unit rate. Agent movement is governed by rule **M** (each agent moves to the nearest unoccupied site having largest sugar within its vision and gathers the sugar) and sex is turned off. In the animations that follow agents are colored according to their group, with Blues colored blue and Reds colored red. A typical cultural evolution of this artificial society is shown in animation III-6.

The animation terminates with all agents Blue after some 2700 time periods. If, as in this run, the initial population segregates spatially—with separate subpopulations hiving separate sugar heights—then each such subpopulation will ultimately converge to pure Blue or pure Red.[22] Thus, **K** is *sufficient to generate* cultural groups.

One way to monitor tag-flipping dynamics is to use a histogram displaying—at each time—the percentage of all agents having 0s at each

---

21. In order to keep this rule unambiguous the number of tags should be odd.

22. For a spatially segregated population engaged in cultural transmission according to rule **K** it can be shown that a monochromatic state is an absorbing state of the process. If some (small) rate of cultural tag mutation is introduced, then the system will hover near one of the monochromatic states, occasionally changing colors completely. Similar dynamics arise in a variety of contexts; see Arthur [1988, 1990], Arthur, Ermoliev, and Kaniovski [1987], and Kaniovski [1994].

Animation III-6. Tag-Flipping Dynamics under Rules ($\{G_1\}$, $\{M, K\}$)

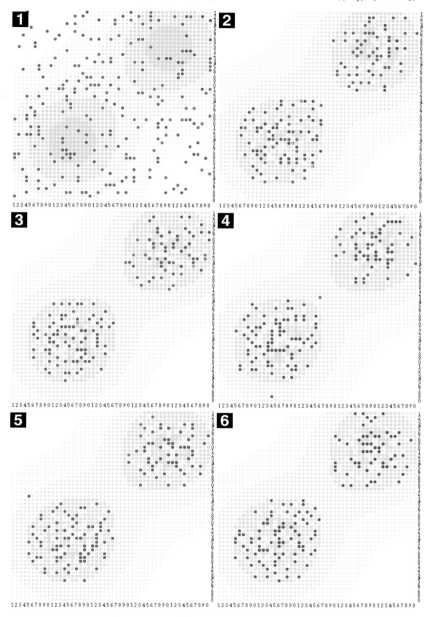

Animation III-7. Tag Histogram Evolution under Rules ({$\mathbf{G}_1$}, {$\mathbf{M}$, $\mathbf{K}$})

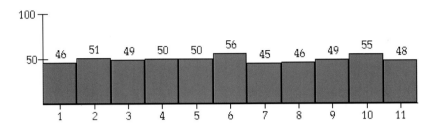

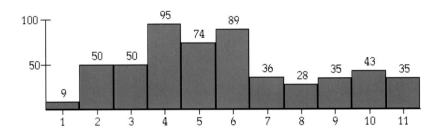

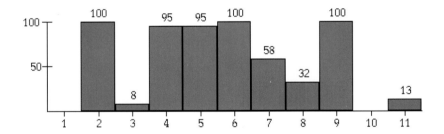

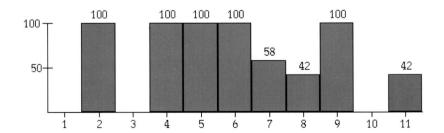

Figure III-8. Typical Cultural Tag Time Series Realization under Rules $(\{\mathbf{G}_1\}, \{\mathbf{M}, \mathbf{K}\})$

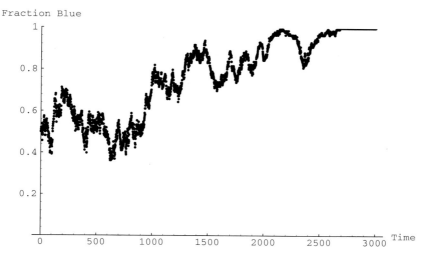

position on the tag string. Suppose we freeze such a histogram at some instant in the tag-flipping process, as shown in the first frame of animation III-7. The horizontal axis is divided into eleven bins, one for each tag position. The height of the bin gives the percentage of agents having a 0 at that position. So, in this example 49 percent initially have a 0 as the third tag of their string, 55 percent have a 0 as the tenth tag, and so forth. Of course, tag-flipping unfolds in time so the histogram is not frozen but evolves as the reader will see by running animation III-7. This dynamic histogram gives tag statistics obtained from the previous animation.

For some tag positions the percentage of all agents having a zero ultimately converges to zero (all agents have a 1 there) or one hundred (all agents have a zero there). Of course, once either of these "unanimous" states is reached, there can be no further tag-flipping since there is no tag diversity at that position. In short, there is "lock-in."

Figure III-8 shows a plot of the fraction of Blue agents over time. Note that long-run convergence to a single group need not be monotonic; wild fluctuations may occur en route to equilibrium. As the length of the cultural chromosome increases, so does the time required for convergence. Similarly, adding agents increases convergence time.

Now, two individuals might each consider themselves "American" culturally, while differing politically, religiously, or in other respects. An interesting feature of this agent group membership rule is that agents can be very different culturally, measured position-by-position, and yet be members of the same group. To see this consider two agents having tag length five. Suppose the first has tag string 00011 and the second has tags 11000. These two agents have but a single tag in common, the third one, and yet they are both Blue since 0s predominate. All agents can be the same color (as in figure III-8) *without* being culturally identical. A corollary of this is that a pair of Blues can produce a Red agent. How can this happen? Imagine a Blue agent (who is the flipper) and a Blue neighbor (the "flippee," as it were) with the following tag strings of length five:

Agent's tag string	10100	Blue
Neighbor's pre-flip tag string	01010	Blue

Each is Blue since 0s outnumber 1s. But suppose "God" (the random number generator) picks tag position three. Since the agent has a 1 there, it flips the neighbor's tag to 1 at that position, resulting in the neighbor's new tag string: 01110. But now 1s outnumber 0s, so the neighbor turns Red! Once more, a simple rule—here the tag-flipping rule—produces interesting results.

Ultimately, we want to have cultural transmission operational at the same time the sex rule is active, so we need some way to specify the state of a newborn child's cultural tags. The transmission of cultural attributes from parents to children is termed *vertical,* as against the *horizontal* transmission we have been discussing.

Vertical Transmission of Culture

When sex rule **S** is active, a child's tag string is formed by comparing the parents' tags at each position and applying the following rule: If the parents have the same tag (both have 0 or both have 1), the child is assigned that tag. If, however, one parent has tag 0 and the other has tag 1, then we "toss a fair coin." If it comes up heads, the child's tag is 1, if tails, it is 0. All of this is summarized in table III-2.[23]

---

23. Those with a background in population genetics will notice that this is strictly analogous to a random mating table for one locus with two alleles.

Table III-2. Probability That a Child Receives a 0 or 1 Tag When Born, Based on the Parents' Tags

	Probability that a child's tag is	
Parents' tags	0	1
Mother 0, father 0	1	0
Mother 0, father 1	1/2	1/2
Mother 1, father 0	1/2	1/2
Mother 1, father 1	0	1

This procedure is applied at each position, resulting in a cultural endowment—a tag string—for every newborn child. Of course, once the child is out on its own all agent behavioral rules apply, including **K**. Thus horizontal transmission will soon modify the child's initial, vertically transmitted, tags.

Networks of Friends

In Chapter II we defined agent neighbor networks and showed how these change over time. Earlier in this chapter we displayed genealogical networks. Here, given that the agents are flipping tags with their neighbors as they move around the sugarscape, a natural notion of "friendship" arises. Agents who at some point are neighbors and are close culturally are defined to be friends.[24] When an agent is born it has no friends. However, in moving around the landscape it meets many agents—as neighbors—and interacts with them culturally. Those agents with whom it interacts and who are closest to it culturally are ones it remembers as its friends.[25] Then, if one draws lines between friends, one has a friendship network.

To implement this in Sugarscape, we employ the Hamming distance to measure the closeness of cultural tag strings.[26] Each agent keeps track of

---

24. We offer this definition of "friendship" as a simple local rule that can be implemented efficiently, not as a faithful representation of current thinking about the basis for human friendship.

25. In the agent object this is implemented as a pointer to the friend agent (see Appendix A for more on the object-oriented implementation of the agents).

26. The Hamming distance between two (equal length) binary strings is obtained by comparing the strings position-by-position and totaling the number of positions at which they are different. Therefore, two strings having a Hamming distance equal to zero are identical.

the five agents it has encountered who are nearest it culturally; these are its friends. Each time an agent encounters a new neighbor the agent determines how close they are culturally and, if the neighbor is closer than any of the agent's five friends, the neighbor displaces one of them. Drawing connections between friends yields the network shown in animation III-8.[27]

Many variants on this general idea are possible.[28] For instance, instead of connecting all friends one could draw lines only between *mutual friends*; that is, a line would connect agents A and B only if A considers B as a friend and *vice versa*. Another variation would be to connect only *best friends*; that is, A must consider B to be its best friend—closest culturally—and B must think the same of A. Finally, note that whether two agents are friends or not has no effect on their behavior. In this sense the network of friends is *external* to either the cultural exchange process or the friend assignment rule. A natural extension of the "network-of-agents" concept would be to permit regular agent-agent interaction over such networks, reinforcing positive interactions and perhaps breaking connections as a result of negative interactions, a kind of Hebbian picture.[29] In this way the networks take on a feedback flavor; interagent cultural transmission begets networks of friends, which in turn modify the transmission dynamics.

Networks such as those we have described manifest themselves in the real world in many important ways. Politically, restrictions on freedom of assembly, freedom of speech (press censorship), and freedom of movement (internal passport requirements) are standard tactics of repressive governments. The main aim of these measures is to keep individual dissenters—of which there may be a great many—isolated from one another, to keep them from *connecting* with other dissenters, and so

---

27. Occasionally a line across the entire lattice is observed. Since the sugarscape is a torus, an agent at the extreme left of the lattice may be a friend of an agent at the extreme right, yielding a friend connection line that spans the entire lattice.

28. There are actually two distinct ways to keep track of friends, producing somewhat different pictures. In animation III-8, once an agent stores another as its friend it never checks to see whether or not the agent continues to be close culturally once the two agents cease to be neighbors. That is, the agent's list of friends can become highly anachronistic as both it and its friends engage in cultural exchange over time. An alternative way to implement friends would be to keep updating the cultural closeness of friends each time period, although this would involve spatially nonlocal communication.

29. Recently Holland [1993] has studied the effects of tags on social interactions in an agent-based model.

Animation III-8. Evolution of a Network of Friends under Rules
($\{\mathbf{G}_1\}$, $\{\mathbf{M}, \mathbf{K}\}$)

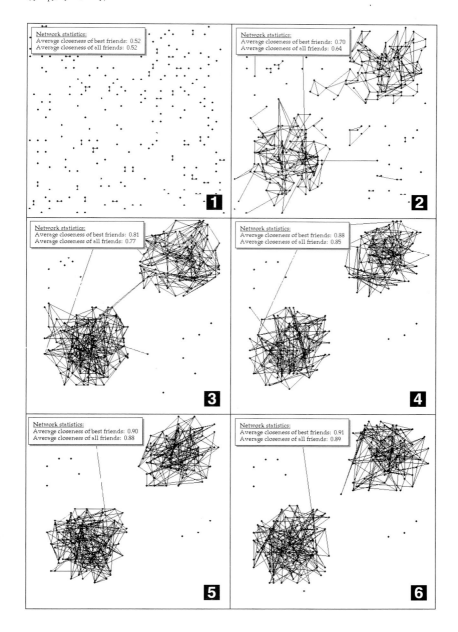

to thwart the emergence of an organized *community* of dissenters, conscious of their numbers. How do changing political borders and "information revolutions" (for example, the Internet) affect the emergence of groups? How does "samizdata" spread across a landscape? Artificial societies allow us to study such questions systematically.

Now that rules for sexual reproduction and cultural exchange have been elaborated, let us turn to combat.

Combat

The cultural processes described above have proved *sufficient to generate* tribes—distinct cultural formations of agents. In this section we permit combat between agents from different tribes.[30] We do this by modifying the movement rule.

Specifically, imagine being a Blue agent. And suppose that within your range of vision there is a lattice position of sugar height 3, and that there is a Red agent sitting at that position. Then, if you take over that position, you take in the 3 sugar units *plus some additional reward from preying upon the Red agent*. One possibility is that you get the total accumulated sugar wealth of the agent. Or you might get a flat reward of, say, 2 sugar units. In the latter case, the full value of taking over the position would be 3 + 2 = 5 sugar units. We will examine both types of reward rules. First, however, we need to establish reasonable conditions under which agents can prey on members of the opposite tribe.

To begin, it does not seem plausible that a "tiny" agent (one with little accumulated sugar) should be able to prey on a "huge" agent (one with vast accumulated sugar). At a minimum, then, we require that the predator be bigger than the prey in terms of accumulated sugar. It turns out that, to produce interesting dynamics, something more is required. In particular, if you are a Blue agent then you can plunder a Red agent—call him Rollo—only on two conditions. First, you must be bigger than Rollo. But second, there must be no other Red agent within your vision bigger than you will be after you defeat Rollo. In that case, we *define* the attack site as being *invulnerable to retaliation*. This second requirement provides

---

30. For an interesting discussion of tribal warfare from an anthropological perspective, see Ferguson [1992].

an element of deterrence, which enriches the dynamics significantly. A formal statement of the combat rule, for any reward α, is as follows:

Agent combat rule C_α:
- Look out as far as vision permits in the four principal lattice directions;
- Throw out all sites occupied by members of the agent's own tribe;
- Throw out all sites occupied by members of different tribes who are wealthier than the agent;
- The reward of each remaining site is given by the resource level at the site plus, if it is occupied, the minimum of α and the occupant's wealth;
- Throw out all sites that are vulnerable to retaliation;
- Select the nearest position having maximum reward and go there;
- Gather the resources at the site plus the minimum of α and the occupant's wealth, if the site was occupied;
- If the site was occupied, then the former occupant is considered "killed"—permanently removed from play.

Note that the rule C_∞ implies that the aggressor receives the full accumulation of the defeated agent.

Reward Equal to Accumulated Wealth

Indeed, in our first combat run we specify that the entire accumulated wealth of the prey goes to the predator; C_∞ is in effect. Allowing infinite lifetimes, predators can accumulate tremendous power under this rule. A type of increasing returns is evident—the bigger you are the faster you grow. Beginning with two separate tribes, social evolution under this reward rule always goes to one of three patterns: Blue eradicates Red, Red eradicates Blue, or small colonies (as small as one agent) of Reds and Blues coexist, each on its own mountain peak. Interestingly, Reds and Blues usually switch mountains in the course of the run. Animation III-9 shows an evolution to Blue dominance.

Starting from different initial conditions, animation III-10 shows an evolution to spatially segregated Blue and Red "colonies," each on its own mountain peak, with a small cluster of low vision Blues subsisting in the lowlands of the southwest.

Animation III-9. Blue Takeover under Rule System ($\{\mathbf{G}_1\}$, $\{\mathbf{C}_\infty\}$)

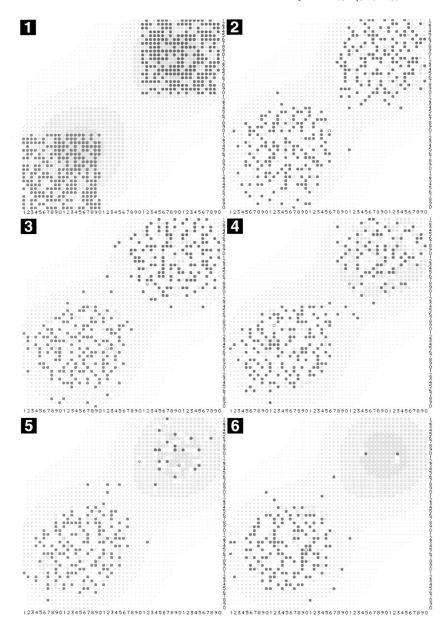

Animation III-10. Red and Blue Coexistence under Rules ($\{\mathbf{G}_1\}$, $\{\mathbf{C}_\infty\}$)

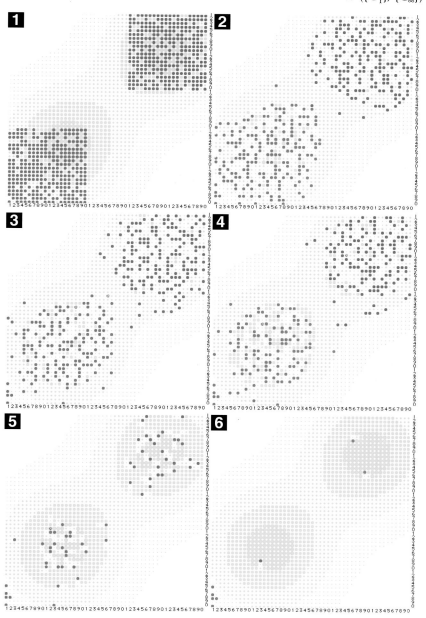

Notice that the mountains have, indeed, changed hands in these runs. In other words, no stable "battle front" emerges under this reward rule. If, however, the reward rule is modified, qualitatively different patterns of conflict become possible.

Reward Equal to a Fixed Value

Here, rather than the entire accumulated wealth of the victim, the conquering agent receives *a fixed sugar reward of 2 sugar units per kill*; that is, the combat rule is C_2. To generate sustained combat between tribes, we fix the population at 400 agents by reintroducing the replacement rule, $R_{[60,100]}$, from Chapter II. Recall that this institutes a maximum lifetime uniformly distributed between 60 and 100 years, and when an agent dies it is replaced by a random agent of the same tribe (one with randomly chosen vision, metabolism, and initial sugar endowment). Animation III-11 shows the result.

Now we *do* get coherent battle fronts. Penetration is minimal and a prolonged "war of attrition" ensues, not the stunning *blitzkrieg* of animation III-9.

Effect of Rule Changes on Emergent Structures

Clearly, *individual* behavior under the combat rule is different from *individual* behavior in the no-combat case. But, how does the prospect of combat affect emergent *collective* structures? Recall, for example, the *collective* waves of animation II-6. An initial block of Blue agents with maximum vision of ten (a relatively high value) propagated in a sequence of northeasterly waves. If we *turn combat off* and begin with opposed blocks of Blue and Red agents—in the southwest and northeast corners of the sugarscape—each population will propagate, again on a diagonal, toward the center in *collective waves that collide and interpenetrate* as shown in animation III-12.

Now, suppose we turn combat on, substituting rule C_α for rule **M**. Do waves still result? Animation III-13, with $\alpha = 2$, gives the answer.

Agents are deterred from racing forward to attack smaller agents of the opposed tribe by the presence of larger opposing agents within their vision. Precisely the factor—relatively high average vision—that produced the waves in the no-combat world now accounts for their absence. To complexity scientists, the moral is clear: When you change local rules, you may change emergent collective structures. For policymakers, there

Animation III-11. "Trench War" under Rules ($\{\mathbf{G}_1\}$, $\{\mathbf{C}_2$, $\mathbf{R}_{[60,100]}\}$)

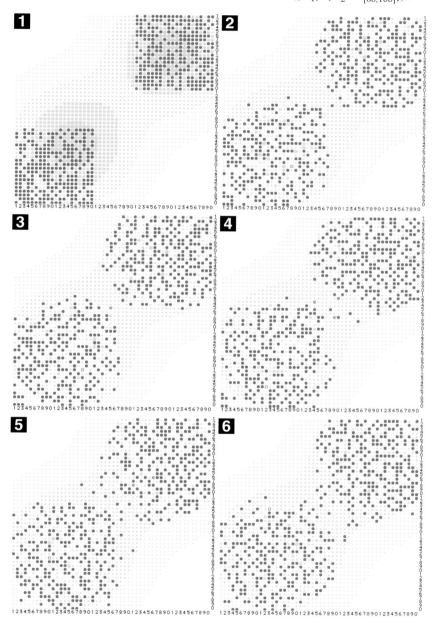

Animation III-12. Colliding Waves under Rules ($\{\mathbf{G}_1\}$, $\{\mathbf{M}\}$)

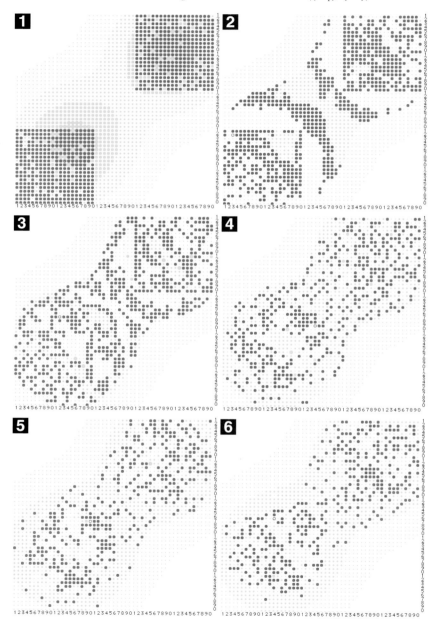

Animation III-13. Combat Eliminates Waves, Rule System ($\{\mathbf{G}_1\}$, $\{\mathbf{C}_2\}$)

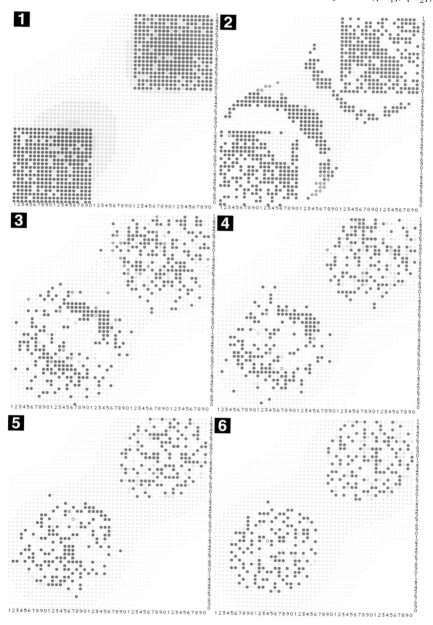

is a corollary: The most effective way to alter collective patterns of behavior may be from the bottom up, by modifying local rules.

Combat and Assimilation: Two Modes of Group Defense

To examine how combat and cultural assimilation (tag-flipping) can interact, recall animation III-9. This was a pure combat simulation, beginning with segregated Red and Blue populations, one on each sugar mountain. The combat reward rule was that a victor acquires *the entire accumulated wealth* of the vanquished agent. In animation III-9 the result was Blue eradication of Red. In particular, we saw that once a sufficiently big Blue agent penetrated Red society, there was no way of stopping it, no way for any individual Red to defeat it in combat. But, what if that Blue invader's tags were being flipped while it was rampaging through Red society? Could the Reds convert it to a Red before it ravaged their society? Let us see. In animation III-14, everything is exactly as in animation III-9 (Blue takeover), except that cultural processes are unfolding.

Now, with cultural exchange processes active we do *not* see the same runaway to hegemony. Although a Blue agent certainly penetrates Red society and (through early combat victories) quickly acquires an insurmountable combat edge over any Red, the Blue invader's cultural tags are all the while being flipped—indeed, precisely because the Blue intruder is surrounded by Reds, the latter will get many opportunities to flip the invader's tags. The defending Reds are in fact able to convert, or assimilate, their attackers before being conquered. Later in this run, the Blue tribe defends itself the same way.

Once a huge invading Blue is converted to Red, it contributes a substantial measure of deterrence to the Red tribe. So, for deterrence, it is best if the big new convert is deployed far forward, close to the threatening Blue hordes. However, since the new convert might be "just barely Red"—by only one or two tags—it is not yet terribly trustworthy; it could easily be flipped back by a patch of neighboring Blues. Of course, before its conversion, the big former Blue might well have penetrated deep into the very center of Red society, where, as a new recruit, its complete ideological conversion—re-education—can proceed without "distraction," as it were. The dynamics, ultimately, depend on the interplay between tag length and the combat reward.

Clearly, the longer the tag string, the longer it will take to convert an intruder. A total fanatic (one with tag string of "infinite" length) can never be converted. By the same token if the combat reward is very modest—say one sugar per kill instead of the entire wealth of the

Animation III-14. Combat and Cultural Transmission, Rule System ($\{\mathbf{G}_1\}$, $\{\mathbf{C}_\infty$, $\mathbf{K}\}$)

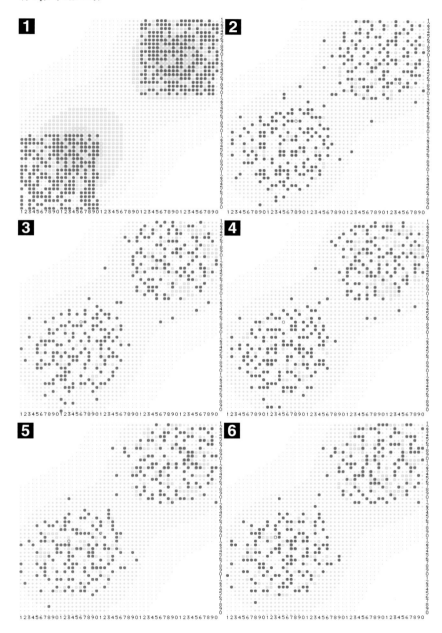

victim—there is much more time for tag-flipping before Blue takeover. In short, these two fundamental modes of group defense—combat and assimilation—trade off in interesting ways.[31]

While each rule of agent behavior discussed thus far—movement, combat, cultural transmission, and reproduction—deserves much more analysis, we have now assembled everything needed to "grow" the promised proto-history.

The Proto-History

The question posed at the start of this chapter was whether we can grow a crude caricature of early social history "from the bottom up" with these ingredients. Recall that the proto-history's main components are the formation of spatially segregated tribes, tribe growth, and tribal interaction. We submit animation III-15 as a realization of the proto-history using the movement (**M**), sexual reproduction (**S**), and cultural (**K**) rules we have now accumulated.

At first there is a small, low density, primordial "soup" of agents with random genetics (vision, metabolism, and so on), random cultural tag strings, and random initial positions on the familiar twin-peaked sugarscape. The fundamental drive for sugar produces migration to one or another of the sugar peaks, and thus spatial segregation into two sub-populations in which mating and cultural transmission occur. And each sub-population converges (culturally) to pure Red or pure Blue; the tribes are formed. Sexual reproduction now increases each tribe's population, forcing Reds and Blues down from their sugar highland origins into the lowlands between. There the tribes interact perpetually, with collisions, penetrations, and conversions producing complex social histories. There are "expansionist" phases in which it looks as if one tribe will achieve hegemony; and there are "epochs" of stalemate, where scattered border contacts and "assimilations" are the rule.[32]

---

31. Formal top-down models of group defense include Freedman and Wolkowicz [1986] and Freedman and Hongshun [1988].

32. This outcome—Red and Blue tribes on opposite mountains—is realized in somewhat less than 1/2 of the runs of the model with rules ($\{G_1\}$, $\{M, S, K\}$) active. In about 1/4 of the runs, Red cultural groups come to dominate both mountains, while Blue domination occurs with the same frequency. (As an aside, recall from animation III-6 that two non-communicating groups may both become Red without having *exactly* the same culture.) It is also the case that extinction on one or both of the mountains occurs with some small frequency.

Animation III-15. A Realization of the Proto-History, Produced by Rules ({**G₁**}, {**M, S, K**})

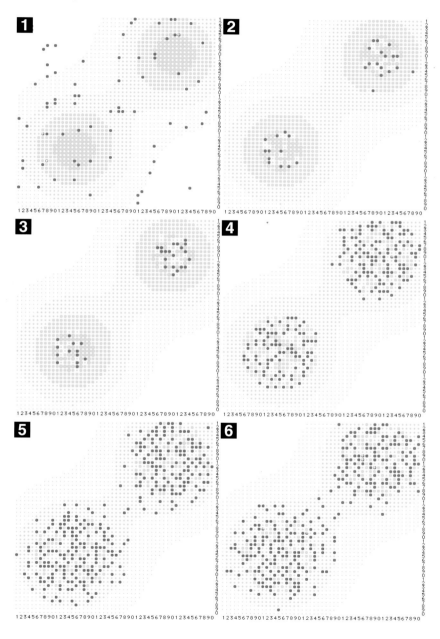

IV

Sugar and Spice:
Trade Comes to the Sugarscape

Like the other animals, we find and pick up what we can use, and appropriate territories. But unlike the other animals, we also trade and produce for trade.
Jane Jacobs, **Systems of Survival** *[1992: xi]*

In the previous chapters we have studied simple agents having local rules for movement, sex, cultural exchange, and combat. In this chapter, we explore another crucial social behavior: *trade*. So far, our methodology has been to postulate one or more agent rules and then study the society that unfolds. Sometimes we presented a "target" social outcome before providing any rules (for example, the "proto-history"), while at other times we argued that the rules themselves were of interest since they were in some sense simple or minimal (for example, the movement rule **M**).

In this chapter, we proceed somewhat differently. We draw on neo-classical microeconomic theory for rules governing agent trade behavior.[1] These rules mediate the interaction of infinitely lived agents who have unchanging, well-behaved preferences that they truthfully reveal to one another and who engage in trade only if it makes them better off (technically, trade must be Pareto-improving). However, instead of the neoclassical stipulation that the agents interact only with the price system—that is, all agents are price-takers—we implement trade as occurring between neighboring agents at prices determined locally by a simple bargaining rule.[2] Individual agents do not use any nonlocal price infor-

---

1. In some agent-based computer simulations the term "trade" is used loosely, to denote any interagent transfer of internal stocks, independent of whether the agents have any internal mechanism for computing the welfare associated with such transfers. This is not a usage of interest to economists.

2. Kirman [1994], in his review of the literature on economies with interacting agents, suggests that "models in which agents interact with each other directly rather than indirectly through the market price mechanism provide a rich and promising class of alternatives which may help us to overcome some of the difficulties of the standard models."

mation in their decisionmaking. Because price formation is local, this is a model of *completely decentralized exchange* between neoclassical agents. Later we relax some of the least realistic aspects of the neoclassical set-up; for example, giving the agents finite lives and nonfixed preferences.

The main issue we address is the extent to which interacting agents are capable of producing *socially optimal* outcomes, that is, allocations of resources having the property that no agent can be made better off through further trade. The artificial societies modeling approach allows us to explore such questions systematically and reproducibly. In particular, we compare the performance of distinct classes of agents—neoclassical agents and various non-neoclassical ones. We find that neoclassical agents trading bilaterally are able to approach, over time, a price close to that associated with an optimal allocation. However, when the agents are made progressively less neoclassical—when they are permitted to sexually reproduce or have culturally varying preferences—the markets that emerge generally have suboptimal performance for indefinite periods of time.

Such results have important implications. First and foremost, the putative case for laissez-faire economic policies is that, left to their own devices, market processes yield equilibrium prices. Individual (decentralized) utility maximization at these prices then induces Pareto optimal allocations of goods and services. But if no price equilibrium occurs, then the efficiency of the allocations achieved becomes an open question and the theoretical case for pure market solutions is weakened.

We also investigate the effect of trade on variables studied in previous chapters. We find that the *carrying capacity* of the resource-scape is increased by trade, but so is the *skewness of the wealth distribution*. More agents exist in a society that engages in trade, but the resulting society is more unequal. Furthermore, the markets that result from our local trade rule generate *horizontal inequality*—agents with identical endowments and preferences end up in different welfare states. Importantly, the welfare theorems of neoclassical economics do not hold in such markets.

When agents are allowed to enter into credit relationships with one another—for purposes of bearing children—interesting financial networks emerge. Some agents end up as pure lenders, others as pure borrowers, and many turn out to be both lenders and borrowers. Indeed, entire financial hierarchies emerge within the agent society.

It seems natural to think of market processes as a form of social computation, with the agents operating as distributed processing "nodes" and the flow of commodities serving as inter-node communication. Each

Figure IV-1. Sugar Mountains in the Northeast and Southwest, Spice in the Northwest and Southeast

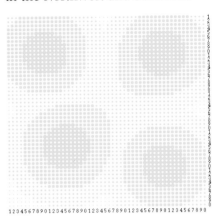

node (agent) executes a local optimization algorithm (purposive behavior), attempting to maximize a local objective (utility) function through decentralized interactions with other nodes (agents). The market as a whole—the social computer—tends toward a globally optimal allocation of goods, as if it were "attempting" to *compute* such an allocation. In this chapter we study how the success of this social computation depends on agent specifications.

Spice: A Second Commodity

To begin, since trade involves an exchange of distinct items between individuals, the first task is to add a second commodity to the landscape. This second resource, "spice," is arranged in two mountains opposite the original sugar mountains, as depicted in figure IV-1.[3] At each position there is a sugar level and capacity, as before, as well as a spice level and capacity.

Each agent now keeps two separate accumulations, one of sugar and one of spice, and has two distinct metabolisms, one for each good. These

---

3. An infinite variety of other arrangements of the resources is possible, of course, and we have experimented with various topographies. However, the configuration depicted in figure IV-1 will be used exclusively here. While the details of particular model runs are intimately intertwined with the economic geography employed, the qualitative character of the results does not depend on any particular topography.

metabolic rates are heterogeneous over the agent population, just as in the single commodity case, and represent the amount of the commodities the agents must consume each period to stay alive. Agents die if *either* their sugar or their spice accumulation falls to zero.

The Agent Welfare Function

We now need a way for the agents to compare their needs for the two goods. A "rational" agent having, say, equal sugar and spice metabolisms but with a large accumulation of sugar and small holdings of spice should pursue sites having relatively more spice than sugar. One way to capture this is to have the agents compute how "close" they are to starving to death due to a lack of either sugar or spice. They then attempt to gather relatively more of the good whose absence most jeopardizes their survival. In particular, imagine that an agent with metabolisms (m_1, m_2) and accumulations (w_1, w_2) computed the "amount of time until death given no further resource gathering" for each resource; these durations are just $\tau_1 \equiv w_1/m_1$ and $\tau_2 \equiv w_2/m_2$. The relative size of these two quantities, the dimensionless number τ_1/τ_2, is a measure of the relative importance of finding sugar to finding spice. A number less than one means that sugar is relatively more important, while a number greater than one means that spice is needed more than sugar.

An agent welfare function giving just these relative valuations at the margins is[4]

$$W(w_1,w_2) = w_1^{m_1/m_T} w_2^{m_2/m_T},\tag{1}$$

where $m_T = m_1 + m_2$. Note that this is a Cobb-Douglas functional form. The metabolisms make an agent's welfare dependent upon its biology in just the way we want; that is, if an agent has a higher metabolism for the first commodity (sugar) than for the second (spice), then it views a site having equal quantities of sugar and spice as if there were relatively less sugar present.

This welfare function is *state-dependent* insofar as the arguments (w_1,w_2) denote accumulated quantities of the two commodities, not instantaneous consumption. This gives the agents the behavioral characteristic that as they age, for example, and accumulate wealth, they

---

4. This will be made precise below in the discussion of "internal valuations."

view the same resource site differently.[5] This state-dependence, while a departure from the utility function usual in neoclassical economics, is a natural way to represent preferences for agents who do not consume their entire commodity bundle each period.

The Agent Movement Rule in the Presence of Two Commodities

Given this welfare function, the movement rule followed by the agents is identical to what it was in the simple one commodity case, namely, look around for the best position and move there. The only difference in the two commodity case is that establishing which location is "best" involves evaluating the welfare function at each prospective site. Let s denote a site, with x_1^s and x_2^s the sugar and spice levels at that site. Formally, the agents perform an optimization calculation over the sites in their vision-parameterized neighborhood, N_v, according to

$$\max_{s \in N_v} W(w_1 + x_1^s, w_2 + x_2^s). \qquad (2)$$

In other words, given an agent with some sugar wealth w_1 and spice wealth w_2, every position within the agent's vision is inspected and the agent calculates what its welfare would be were it to go there and collect the sugar and spice. Expression (2) says simply that the agent selects the site producing maximum welfare.[6] As in the case of a single commodity, if there are several sites that produce equal welfare then the first site encountered is selected. Overall, the new movement rule for each agent is as follows.

Multicommodity agent movement rule **M**:[7]
- Look out as far as vision permits in each of the four lattice directions, north, south, east, and west;

---

5. Derivations in Appendix C give formal conditions under which an agent facing identical (distributions of) resource levels at distinct times in its life will rank sites differently due solely to changes in its wealth.

6. It is possible to unify the one and two commodity cases conceptually by imagining that in the former case the agents are "optimizing" a welfare function that has just one argument; that is,

$$W(w;m) = w^m.$$

7. We use **M** to symbolize all variants of the movement rule. In the Sugarscape software system the number of commodities, n, is a user-adjustable parameter, and so **M** has actually been implemented as the n-dimensional analog of expression (2).

- Considering only unoccupied lattice positions, find the nearest position producing maximum welfare;
- Move to the new position;
- Collect all the resources at that location.

Now we study how the addition of the second commodity affects individual movement dynamics. To see that the effect is profound, one need only look at a particular run of the model, such as animation IV-1. Here vision is uniformly distributed in the agent population between 1 and 10, while metabolism for each of the two commodities is uniformly distributed between 1 and 5. A black tail is attached to one arbitrarily chosen agent, a so-called observational agent, to highlight the complexity of individual trajectories.

The agents search locally for the spot that makes them best off and they move there. However, because of the spatial separation of the two resources, agents move back and forth between the two types of mountains: Staying on one mountain for an extended period of time augments the agent's holdings of one commodity but dissipates its holdings of the other, forcing it to migrate. Note that if one were to average the observational agent's location over time its mean position would fall somewhere between the two types of mountains, despite the fact that the agent spends precious little time at such locations. That is, spatio-temporal averaging gives us little understanding of actual agent behavior.

The *carrying capacity* of this landscape is lower than in the single commodity (sugar-only) case, because there are now *two* ways to die, namely, by running out of *either* resource. A common route to death on the two-resource landscape is for an agent to run low on one of the resources while "stocking up" on the other and then find itself in a region of the resource-scape where there is a low density (and a flat gradient) of the needed good: having eaten its way deep into a high sugar (low spice) zone, the agent dies of spice deprivation, for example. Most agents in animation IV-1 never suffer this fate. When spice depletion threatens they have sufficient vision to find spice rich zones and replenish their stocks. Of course, there is another way agents might obtain commodities they need: through trade.[8]

---

8. Below we show that the general effect of trade is indeed to *augment* the carrying capacity.

Animation IV-1. Elaborate Trajectory of an "Observational" Agent in the Case of Both Sugar and Spice Present under Rule System $(\{\mathbf{G}_1\}, \{\mathbf{M}\})$

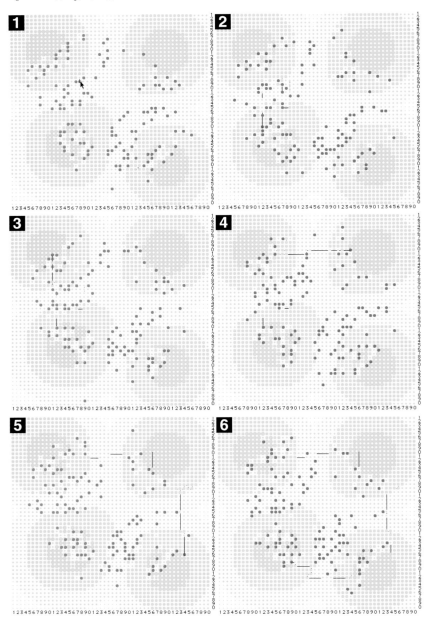

Trade Rules

Permitting agents to trade requires a rule system for the exchange of sugar and spice between agents.[9] When will agents trade? How much will they trade? And at what price will exchange occur? There are a variety of ways in which to proceed.

The neoclassical theory of general equilibrium describes how a single centralized market run by a so-called auctioneer can arrive at an equilibrium price vector for the entire economy—a set of prices at which all markets clear. The image of an auctioneer announcing prices to the entire economy is quite unrealistic; no individual or institution could ever possess either complete knowledge of agent preferences and endowments or sufficient computational power to determine the appropriate prices. And even if market-clearing prices were somehow identified, why would all agents use them, why would all agents be price-takers?[10]

A more recognizable image is presented by Kreps [1990: 196], under the heading "Why (not) Believe in Walrasian Equilibrium?" He writes:

> . . . we can imagine consumers wandering around a large market square, with all their possessions on their backs. They have chance meetings with each other, and when two consumers meet, they examine what each has to offer, to see if they can arrange a mutually agreeable trade. . . . If an exchange is made, the two swap goods and wander around in search of more advantageous trades made at chance meetings.

We implement trade in precisely this fashion, as welfare-improving (that is, mutually agreeable) bilateral barter between agents. No use is made of an auctioneer or any similar artifice. Agents move around the resource-scape following **M**, but are now permitted to trade with the agents they land next to, that is, their von Neumann neighbors. When an agent-neighbor pair interacts to trade, the process begins by having each agent compute its internal valuations of sugar and spice. Then a

---

9. Since there is no money in our artificial society, it is perhaps more accurate to describe interagent trade as barter. Throughout this chapter we shall use the terms "trade," "exchange," and "barter" interchangeably. On the emergence of money in an agent-based model see Marimon, McGrattan, and Sargent [1990].

10. That is, if certain groups of agents can engage in welfare-improving trade *between themselves* at prices other than the market-clearing ones, why would they not do so? Such advantageous reallocations of endowments have been studied by Guesnerie and Laffont [1978].

bargaining process is conducted and a price is agreed to. Finally an exchange of goods between agents occurs if both agents are made better off by the exchange. This process is repeated until no further gains from trade are possible.[11] We now present the details of this process.

Internal Valuations

According to microeconomic theory, an agent's internal valuations of economic commodities are given by its so-called marginal rate of substitution (*MRS*) of one commodity for another. An agent's *MRS* of spice for sugar is the *amount* of spice the agent considers to be as valuable as one unit of sugar, that is, the *value* of sugar in units of spice.[12] For the welfare function (1) above, the *MRS* can be shown to be

$$MRS \equiv \frac{dw_2}{dw_1} = \frac{\frac{\partial W(w_1,w_2)}{\partial w_1}}{\frac{\partial W(w_1,w_2)}{\partial w_2}} = \frac{\frac{m_1}{m_T}w_1^{(m_1-m_T)/m_T}w_2^{m_2/m_T}}{\frac{m_2}{m_T}w_1^{m_1/m_T}w_2^{(m_2-m_T)/m_T}} = \frac{m_1 w_2}{m_2 w_1} = \frac{\frac{w_2}{m_2}}{\frac{w_1}{m_1}} = \frac{\tau_2}{\tau_1}. \quad (3)$$

Note from (3) that an agent's *MRS* depends in an essential way on its metabolisms, that is, its biology. Earlier we noted that the quantities τ_1 and τ_2 represented the times to death by sugar and spice starvation, respectively, assuming no further resource gathering. These quantities are also measures of the *relative internal scarcity* of the two resources, in

---

11. Because our agents trade at nonequilibrium prices this is a non-Walrasian model. In particular, it is a kind of Edgeworth barter process (Negishi [1961], Uzawa [1962], Hahn [1962], and Mukherji [1974]; see Arrow and Hahn [1971: Chapter 13], Hahn [1982], and Fisher [1983: 29-31] for reviews). However, the bilateral nature of our model makes it more completely decentralized than the usual Edgeworth process since prices will generally be heterogeneous during each round of trading. The model closest to ours is Albin and Foley [1990], in which agents maintain fixed positions on a circle and trade with their neighbors. Other non-tâtonnment models include Aubin [1981], Benninga [1992], Feldman [1973], Hey [1974], Lengwiler [1994], Smale [1976], Stacchetti [1985], Walker [1984], and the simulation study of Takayasu *et al.* [1992]. Models of decentralized exchange in which the role of money is studied include Eckalbar [1984, 1986], Friedman [1979], Kiyotaki and Wright [1989, 1991], Madden [1976], Marimon, McGrattan, and Sargent [1990], Menger [1892], Norman [1987], Ostroy and Starr [1974, 1990], and Starr [1976]. Stochastic models of exchange include Bhattacharya and Majumdar [1973], Föllmer [1974], Garman [1976], Keisler [1986, 1992, 1995, 1996], Hurwicz, Radner, and Reiter [1975a, 1975b], and Mendelson [1985]. There is a growing literature of models in which economic agents interact directly with neighbors; for example, see An and Kiefer [1992], Anderlini and Ianni [1993a, 1993b], Ellison [1992], Kiefer, Ye, and An [1993], and Herz [1993].

12. Technically, the *MRS* is the local slope of the sugar-spice indifference curve.

the sense that an agent whose $MRS < 1$, for example, thinks of itself as being relatively poor in spice.

When two agents, A and B, encounter one another—that is, when one moves into the other's neighborhood—the MRS of each agent is computed. Here we treat these internal valuations as common knowledge; that is, the agents truthfully reveal their preferences to one another. If $MRS_A > MRS_B$ then agent A considers sugar to be relatively more valuable than does agent B, and so A is a sugar buyer and a spice seller while agent B is the opposite.[13] The general conditions are summarized in table IV-1. As long as the MRSs are not the same there is potential for trade; that is, one or both of the agents may be made better off through exchange.

Table IV-1. Relative MRSs and the Directions of Resource Exchange

	$MRS_A > MRS_B$		$MRS_A < MRS_B$	
Action	A	B	A	B
Buys	sugar	spice	spice	sugar
Sells	spice	sugar	sugar	spice

The Bargaining Rule and Local Price Formation

Having established the *direction* in which resources will be exchanged, it remains to specify a rule for establishing the *quantities* to be exchanged. The ratio of the spice to sugar quantities exchanged is simply the *price*. This price must, of necessity, fall in the range $[MRS_A, MRS_B]$. To see this, consider the case of two agents, A and B, for whom $MRS_A > MRS_B$. Since A will acquire sugar from B in exchange for spice (see table IV-1), its MRS will, according to (3), decrease as a result of the exchange, while B's MRS will increase. But A will not give up spice for sugar at just any price. Rather, the most spice it is willing to give up for a unit of sugar is precisely its MRS; for one unit of sugar it is willing to trade any amount of spice *below* the quantity given by the MRS. Analogously for B: it is willing to trade at any price *above* its MRS. Thus the range of feasible prices is $[MRS_A, MRS_B]$.

A rule for specifying exchange quantities, and therefore price, might

---

13. Note that whether a particular agent is a sugar buyer or seller is completely endogenous—it depends on the MRS of the other agent with whom the exchange interaction occurs.

be called a *bargaining rule* since it can be interpreted as the (adaptive) way in which two goal-seeking agents instantiate a price from the range of feasible prices.[14] While all prices within the feasible range are "agreeable" to the agents, not all prices appear to be equally "fair." Prices near either end of the range would seem to be a better deal for one of the agents, particularly when the price range is *very* large. Following Albin and Foley [1990], we use as the exchange price the *geometric mean* of the endpoints of the feasible price range. That is, the trading price, p, is determined according to

$$p(MRS_A, MRS_B) = \sqrt{MRS_A MRS_B}. \qquad (4)$$

The primary result of this rule is to moderate the effect of two agents having vastly different MRSs.[15] It turns out that it is more natural to work with $\pi = \ln(p)$, and in describing our artificial economy below we shall compute statistics for π.[16]

Finally, with the price determined, we need to specify the actual quantities of sugar and spice to be exchanged. Here we add the element of indivisibility by stipulating that each exchange involve unit quantity of one of the commodities. In particular, for $p > 1$, p units of spice are exchanged for 1 unit of sugar. If $p < 1$, then 1 unit of spice is exchanged for $1/p$ units of sugar.

The Trade Algorithm

Given that two agents have "bargained to" a price, and thereby specified the quantities to be exchanged, the trade only goes forward if it makes both agents better off. That is, trade must improve the welfare of both agents. Furthermore, since discrete quantities are being traded, and

---

14. There exists an enormous literature on bilateral bargaining when agents have incomplete information. A good introduction is Osborne and Rubinstein [1990], while important papers are reprinted in Linhart, Radner, and Satterthwaite [1992]; see also Gale [1986a, 1986b] and Binmore and Dasgupta [1987]. Since our agents truthfully reveal their preferences we do not make use of these ideas here. Clearly this is an important topic for future work.

15. We have also experimented with a bargaining rule that simply picks a random number from the interval $[MRS_A, MRS_B]$. The qualitative character of the results reported below is insensitive to this change.

16. To see this, note that trading 10 units of spice for one sugar (p = 10) should be treated as equally distant from p = 1 as trading 10 sugars for one spice (p = 1/10). With p = ln(p), this requirement is met since ln(10) - ln(1) = ln(1) - ln(1/10).

therefore repeated exchange may never lead to identical agent *MRS*s, special care must be taken to avoid infinite loops in which a pair of agents alternates between being buyers and sellers of the same resource upon successive application of the trade rule. This is accomplished by forbidding the *MRS*s to cross over one another.[17] Putting all this together we have:[18]

<u>Agent trade rule **T**</u>:
- Agent and neighbor compute their *MRS*s; if these are equal then end, else continue;
- The direction of exchange is as follows: spice flows from the agent with the higher *MRS* to the agent with the lower *MRS* while sugar goes in the opposite direction;
- The geometric mean of the two *MRS*s is calculated—this will serve as the price, p;
- The quantities to be exchanged are as follows: if $p > 1$ then p units of spice for 1 unit of sugar; if $p < 1$ then $1/p$ units of sugar for 1 unit of spice;
- If this trade will (a) make both agents better off (increases the welfare of both agents), and (b) not cause the agents' *MRS*s to cross over one another, then the trade is made and return to start, else end.

Note that the bargaining rule constitutes step 3 of the algorithm.[19]

For a graphical interpretation of **T**, consider the so-called Edgeworth box shown in figure IV-2. Here agent A has sugar-spice endowment of (5, 8), while agent B possesses (15, 2). The red line intersects A's endowment and is A's line of constant utility; that is, A is indifferent between its endowment and all other sugar-spice allocations on the red line. Any allocation below this line is unacceptable to A since such an allocation would yield less welfare than A enjoys at its present position. All allocations above the isoutility line are preferred by A to its current allocation.

---

17. That is, given $MRS_A >(<) MRS_B$, agents stop trading if one additional trade will make $MRS_A <(>) MRS_B$.

18. Heretofore, we have described all rules for the agents and the sugarscape as "simple local rules." We would like it if the trade algorithm **T** could also be described in this way, but realize that one can reasonably say that this rule, although completely local, is hardly simple (requiring, for example, partial differentiation, computation of square roots, and so on). Perhaps it is better described as being the simplest local rule in the neoclassical spirit.

19. It is possible to substitute other bargaining rules simply by replacing this step.

Figure IV-2. Edgeworth Box Representation of Two Agents Trading according to Rule **T**

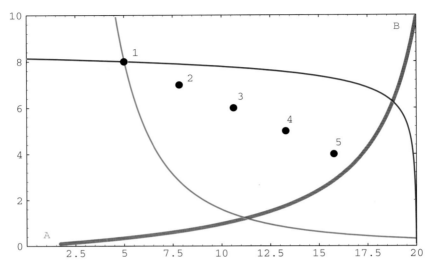

Analogously, B prefers allocations that are below the blue line, its isoutility curve. From any initial endowments we can draw A's and B's isoutility curves. For some endowments the area between the curves will be larger than that shown in figure IV-2, while for others it will be smaller. When initial endowments fall on the gray line, the so-called contract curve, the agents' isoutility curves are exactly tangent—the *MRS*s of the two agents coincide. At these positions there is zero area between the agents' isoutility curves and, as a result, there are no potential gains from trade.[20]

From point 1, each application of rule **T** moves the agents to progressively higher welfare states, first to position 2, then to 3, and so on until finally they reach position 5. Additional trading, beyond 5, would cause the agents' *MRS*s to cross over, and so is not allowed.[21] When **T** results in allocations for agents A and B that are on the contract curve, we say

---

20. For a detailed discussion of the Edgeworth box, see Kreps [1990: 152–53, 155–56].

21. One might reasonably wonder why we have built **T** to take only incremental steps toward the contract curve, instead of jumping directly to it. One rationale is to limit the complexity of our agents; in making small welfare improving trades they use only the local shape of their welfare function in the vicinity of their endowment. They then make a relatively small trade and recompute their marginal valuations with respect to their new holdings.

that *local Pareto optimality* has been achieved.[22] When the allocations produced by **T** are just off the contract curve, as in figure IV-2, we say that near Pareto optimality has been attained locally.

Rule **T** specifies *how* two agents interact to trade. It remains to specify *which* agents interact through **T**. All the rules of agent interaction that we have described so far—rules for sexual reproduction, for cultural interchange—involve local interaction, and here we shall not deviate from this pure bottom-up approach. When an agent following **M** moves to a new location it has from 0 to 4 (von Neumann) neighbors. It interacts through **T** exactly once with each of its neighbors, selected in random order.[23]

The Sugarscape interagent trade rule can be summarized as follows: If neighboring agents have different marginal rates of substitution then they attempt to arrange an exchange that makes them both better off. Bargaining proceeds and a trade price is "agreed" to. Quantities of sugar and spice in proportion to the trade price are specified for exchange. If exchange of the commodities will not cause the agents' *MRS*s to cross over then the transaction occurs, the agents recompute their *MRS*s, and bargaining begins anew. In this way nearly Pareto optimal allocations are produced locally.

With these micro-rules in place we are now in a position to study the aggregate or market behavior of neoclassical agents engaged in bilateral trade. How will prices evolve in such markets? Will trade volumes vary regularly or erratically? Rule **T** stipulates that individual agents are made better off through trade, but will the society of agents *as a whole* be able to extract the full welfare benefits of trade? How sensitive will market performance be to neoclassical assumptions about agents? These are the questions to which we now turn.

---

22. In this usage local Pareto optimality is synonymous with pairwise or bilateral Pareto optimality; see Feldman [1973] and Goldman and Starr [1982].

23. A variant of this would let an agent engage in **T** with a neighboring agent multiple times during a single move. For example, say an agent has 2 neighbors and trades with one of them according to **T**, that is, until they have approximately equal *MRS*s. Then the agent turns to the other neighbor and interacts with it following **T**. After the second set of trades is complete the agent's *MRS* will be different from what it was at the termination of trade with the first neighbor, and therefore it may be feasible to trade further with this first neighbor. The agent is permitted to do so, and it switches back and forth between its neighbors until no more gains from trade are possible. In this variant, the active agent would act as a kind of arbitrageur between its two neighbors.

Markets of Bilateral Traders

General equilibrium theory describes how a centralized market run by an idealized auctioneer can arrive at an equilibrium price. The immediate question for us—having banished the auctioneer and all other types of nonlocal information—is *whether our population of spatially distributed neoclassical agents can produce anything like an equilibrium price through local interactions alone.* It turns out that there is a definite sense in which they can! However, the character of the equilibrium achieved by our agents is rather different from that of general equilibrium theory, for the markets which result produce less than optimal agent welfare—the potential gains from trade are not fully extracted—despite essential convergence to the general equilibrium price. Furthermore, when we relax certain neoclassical assumptions (infinitely lived agents, fixed preferences) overall market performance is further degraded.

Neoclassical Agents and Statistical Price Equilibrium

On the sugar-spice landscape we randomly place a population of 200 infinitely lived agents, having Cobb-Douglas utility functions given by (1), with behavioral rules **M** and **T**. Metabolisms for sugar and spice are uniformly distributed in the agent population between 1 and 5. This has the effect of making preferences symmetrical, that is, there are as many agents who prefer sugar to spice as there are who prefer the reverse. Vision is also uniformly distributed between 1 and 5. Initial endowments are randomly distributed between 25 and 50 for both sugar and spice and are thus also symmetrical with respect to the two resources. Therefore, since there is approximately the same amount of sugar and spice present on the landscape, the symmetry of preferences and endowments implies that the general equilibrium price of sugar to spice will be about 1, varying somewhat from time period to time period.[24]

To display the economic behavior of our artificial market, it would not do to simply "look down from above" on the landscape of agents, as in past animations, since this fails to depict either the formation of prices or the exchange of goods. Instead, we track the time series of average trade price per period.[25] Such a plot is shown in figure IV-3.

---

24. Below we investigate how the general equilibrium price varies, and plot the dynamic supply and demand curves for our artificial economy.

25. We use the phrases "average trade price" and "mean price" to denote the geometric mean of all trade prices that occur in a given period.

Figure IV-3. Typical Time Series for Average Trade Price under Rule System (({**G**₁}, {**M**, **T**})

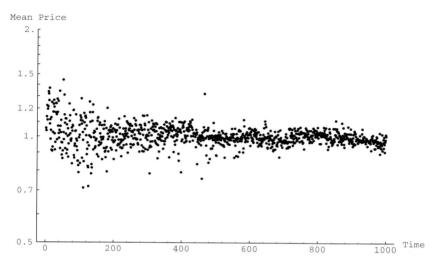

Note that initially there is significant variation in prices but that over time prices tend to bunch around the "market-clearing" level of 1. The total volume of trade is quite large, with nearly 150,000 trades occurring over the time shown in figure IV-3. There is extensive variation in trade volume per period, as shown in figure IV-4. Trade volumes are distributed approximately lognormally, with a few big trade periods and lots of smaller ones.[26]

Another way to look at how prices converge toward the general equilibrium level is to plot the standard deviation in the logarithm of the average trade price per period. For the previous run, this is shown in figure IV-5. Here, and in all subsequent plots of price standard deviation time series, raw data are shown in black with smoothed data in red.

While the standard deviation in price never vanishes, it does tend to stabilize at a relatively small value, averaging about 0.05 by t = 1000.[27] In this case it would seem unobjectionable to say that a price equilibrium is essentially attained by this market. *Economic equilibrium emerges from the bottom up.*

---

26. Actually, the distribution of trade volume is nonstationary when agent lifetimes are infinite.

27. Because agents are infinitely lived in this run of the model, the standard deviation in price will never reach a stationary value but will continue to fall.

Figure IV-4. Typical Time Series of Trade Volume under Rule System ({**G**$_1$}, {**M**, **T**})

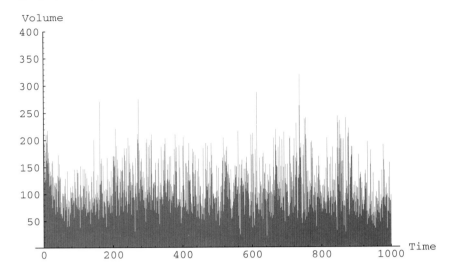

Figure IV-5. Typical Time Series for the Standard Deviation in the Logarithm of Average Trade Price under Rule System ({**G**$_1$}, {**M**, **T**})

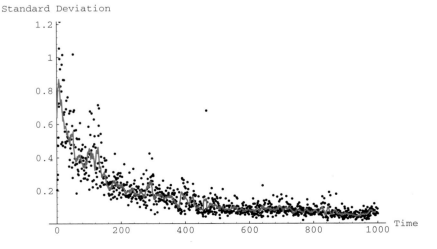

The Invisible Hand

There is a sense in which this completely decentralized, distributed achievement of economic equilibrium is a *more* powerful result than is offered by general equilibrium theory, since *dynamics* of price formation are fully accounted for, and there is no recourse to a mythical auctioneer. This result harks back to Adam Smith and the classical economists whose image of markets involved no such entity.[28]

Performance of Markets Produced by Neoclassical Traders

Having seen typical price-volume time series for markets of neoclassical agents engaged in bilateral trade, we now investigate the nature of these markets.

Carrying Capacity Is Increased by Trade

In Chapter II we found that the notion of *carrying capacity* emerged naturally on the sugarscape.[29] Here we study the effect of trade on the carrying capacity. We do this by noting the number of agents who survive in the long run, first with trade turned off, then with it turned on. Figure IV-6 is a plot of the dependence of carrying capacity on average agent vision, the lower line representing the no-trade case, the upper line the with-trade case.

Clearly, trade *increases* the carrying capacity. This result is in accord with intuition. It was argued earlier that trade was a way for agents to avoid death due to a deficiency in one commodity. To see how this is so, imagine a pair of neighboring agents. Agent 1 has an abundance of sugar but is close to death by spice deprivation; Agent 2 has a surfeit of spice but is on the verge of death through sugar deprivation. If trade is forbidden then each will die. Clearly, however, an exchange of Agent 1's sugar for Agent 2's spice will keep both alive. This is how trade increases the carrying capacity of the sugar-spice scape.

Let us now discuss the nature of the equilibrium produced by com-

---

28. It is usual in economics to associate the Smithian invisible hand with welfare properties of markets, and we do this below. Our usage here has more in common with what Nozick [1974, 1994] calls an "invisible-hand process." For an excellent discussion of Smith's varied usage of the term "invisible hand," see Rothschild [1994].

29. In figure II-5 we presented the dependence of carrying capacity on vision and metabolism distributions in the agent population. As average vision increased and mean metabolism decreased, the carrying capacity increased.

Figure IV-6. Carrying Capacity as a Function of Mean Agent Vision, with and without Trade, under Rule System ($\{\mathbf{G_1}\}, \{\mathbf{M, T}\}$)

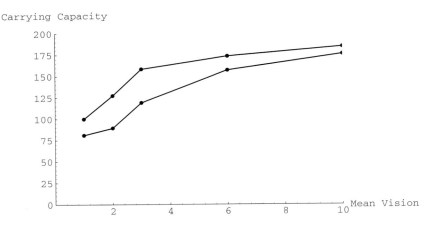

pletely decentralized trade. It is of a profoundly different character than the Walrasian general equilibrium.

Statistical Equilibrium

The equilibrium concept used in general equilibrium theory is a deterministic one. That is, once the auctioneer announces the market-clearing price vector, all agents trade at exactly these prices. Each agent ends up with an allocation that cannot be improved upon. That is, a Pareto-optimal set of allocations obtains. Because these allocations are optimal, no further trading occurs and the economy is said to be in equilibrium. Overall, equilibrium happens in a single trade step.[30]

In the model of bilateral exchange described above, each agent trades not at the general equilibrium price but rather at a locally negotiated one. Imagine that it is some particular agent's turn to move, and you must predict the exact price at which its next trade will occur. This price depends not only on that agent's own internal valuation (*MRS*) but also on that of its trading partner. Predicting the actual trade price involves predicting who this neighbor is likely to be, that agent's *MRS*, and so on. With anything less than a complete description of the entire state space of the artificial society, this calculation can only be made probabilistically.

Recently, Foley [1994] has advanced a novel theory of statistical eco-

---

30. For a classic exposition, see Arrow and Hahn [1971].

nomic equilibrium that has much in common with economic behavior observed in our model.[31] He has argued that general equilibrium theory is "methodologically too ambitious" in that it attempts to compute the allocation for each agent exactly. Indeed, such computations would seem intractable in the relatively simple case of our artificial economy, to say nothing of the real world.

This brings us to the so-called First Welfare Theorem of neoclassical economics.[32] This result is the foundation for economists' claims that markets allocate goods to their optimal social uses. The theorem states that Walrasian equilibria are Pareto-efficient. They are states in which *no reallocation exists such that an agent can be made better off without making at least one other agent worse off*. But in statistical equilibrium

> the First Welfare Theorem should be revised to say that a market equilibrium approximates but cannot achieve a Pareto-efficient allocation. How close a given market comes to Pareto-efficiency can be measured by the price dispersion in transactions. [Foley 1994: 343]

It is exactly this price dispersion that we studied above and will investigate further below in the context of non-neoclassical agents. Thus the philosophical underpinning for laissez-faire policies appears to be weak for markets that display statistical equilibrium.[33]

Horizontal Inequality

Foley [1994] has introduced the term *horizontal inequality* to describe the fact that agents having identical abilities (vision in our model), preferences (parameterized by metabolism in Sugarscape), and endowments will generally have different welfare levels in statistical equilibrium, a phenomenon that is strictly prohibited in Walrasian general equilibrium.

> Differences in final consumption and welfare in Walrasian competitive equilibrium always correspond to differences in initial endowments. But trading at different price ratios leads agents with the same initial endowments to different consumption and utility levels. [Foley 1994: 342]

---

31. This is to be distinguished from the theory of stochastic general equilibrium under incomplete information; for a review see Radner [1982].

32. See Varian [1984: 198–203] for the welfare properties of Walrasian equilibria.

33. The First Welfare Theorem is commonly referred to as the "invisible hand theorem" [Stokey and Lucas 1989: 451–54]. This suggests that decentralized trade must arrive—as if "led by an invisible hand" [Smith 1976: 456]—at Walrasian equilibrium. Our market of decentralized trade certainly does not arrive there.

In other words, the welfare properties of neoclassical general equilibrium markets are *not* preserved in statistical equilibrium, due to the production of horizontal inequality. So once again the *character* of the equilibrium in our model turns out to differ markedly from that in the orthodox theory of general equilibrium.[34] In fact, we expect the production of horizontal inequality to occur in proportion to the variance or dispersion in price in statistical equilibrium. Later it will be shown that such dispersion can be very large indeed.

Local Efficiency, Global Inefficiency

The statistical character of the *price* equilibrium produced by bilateral trade algorithm **T** is very different from the usual general equilibrium notion. It is also true that the *quantities* traded are always different from those that would obtain were the system in general equilibrium. To see this we can make a supply-demand plot for our artificial economy. This is done by querying individual agents as to the quantity of sugar each is willing to supply or demand at a given price. Summing these quantities yields the aggregate supply and demand schedules. The general equilibrium price and quantity can then be computed by interpolation and compared (noiselessly) to the actual (average) trade price and (total) quantity exchanged. Furthermore, these computations can be repeated each period and animated. This is done in animation IV-2 for an artificial economy like the one described in figures IV-3, IV-4, and IV-5.

Notice that while the actual price moves around the general equilibrium price, the actual quantity traded is *always less* than what is necessary to "clear the market." Since agents are unable to trade with anyone other than their neighbors, there is always some "pent-up" demand that goes unfulfilled. That is, if the agents were perfectly mixed, they would engage in additional trades beyond what they achieve through **T**. Over time, as the agents move around, they do meet and interact with these other agents. However, as they move they are accumulating additional goods that they are willing to trade, thus shifting the equilibrium fur-

---

34. The Second Welfare Theorem of neoclassical economics, like the first one, needs to be modified in statistical equilibrium. It states that any Pareto-efficient allocation can be achieved by a Walrasian equilibrium price vector given an appropriate reallocation of endowments. However, in statistical equilibrium

> unless the [initial] endowment can be redistributed directly to the Pareto-efficient allocation, in which case there is nothing for the market to do, the generation of endogenous horizontal inequality among agents appears to be an inescapable by-product of the allocation of resources through decentralized markets. [Foley 1994: 343]

Animation IV-2. Evolution of Supply and Demand under Rule System ($\{\mathbf{G}_1\}$, $\{\mathbf{M}, \mathbf{T}\}$)

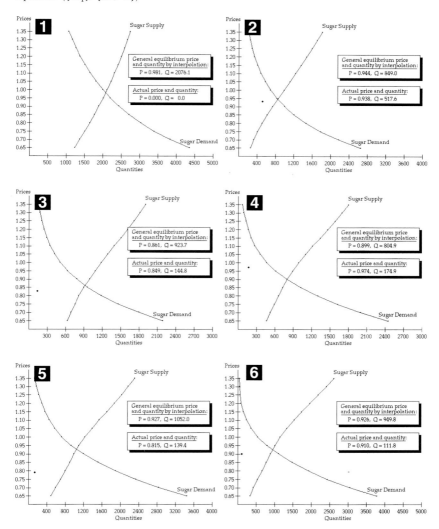

ther. The decentralized economy is always far from general equilibrium in this sense.[35]

This result is of prime significance. For whenever the actual trade volumes are less than the general equilibrium ones, agent society is not extracting all the welfare from trade that it might. If the agents could coordinate their activities beyond their local neighborhoods they could all be made better off. Here we see that *even though T produces exchanges that are nearly Pareto-optimal locally, the resulting market has far from optimal welfare properties globally.*[36]

Far from Equilibrium Economics

A very general principle is lurking here. At each time step agents engage in production (resource gathering according to **M**) and consumption activities as well as pure exchange with their neighbors according to **T**. Because the exchange rule requires time to reach an equilibrium societal allocation, it essentially gives production and consumption time to alter the equilibrium to which **T** is converging. That is, as production and consumption modify endowments they also modify the target the exchange process is trying to achieve. The result is that the economy is far from equilibrium in a very definite sense. These circumstances—exchange taking time to converge while production and consumption constantly shift the equilibrium—are *sufficient* conditions for the existence of a nonequilibrium economy.[37]

---

35. In animation IV-2 there is an increase in both the actual trade volume and the general equilibrium volume over time (the former always lagging the latter). This nonstationarity is due to the infinite livedness of the agents.

36. The far-from-equilibrium character of this spatially distributed market is an interesting result from the perspective of prices as signals appropriate for decentralizing decision-making. Although the market has not reached general equilibrium it is essentially generating the general equilibrium price (though our agents, following **T**, do not use this signal). There are at least two implications of this. First, "getting the price right" is not sufficient to guarantee allocative efficiency. The second conclusion is of a different character. In certain markets it may be that agents use local information exclusively in their economic decisionmaking. In such markets aggregate data such as average prices, a primary focus of economists' attentions, are simply emergent statistically from micro-heterogeneity and of no particular interest to the agents.

37. Fisher [1983: 14] makes a similar point: "In a real economy . . . trading, as well as production and consumption, goes on out of equilibrium. It follows that, in the course of convergence to equilibrium (assuming that occurs), endowments change. In turn this changes the set of equilibria. Put more succinctly, the set of equilibria is path dependent— it depends not merely on the initial state but on the dynamic adjustment process . . . .

Effect of the Distribution of Agent Vision on Price Variance

In figure IV-5 the variance in trade price decays to a relatively small value. Initially, the agents' endowments may have little to do with their preferences (since both endowments and preferences are randomly assigned). Hence, when they encounter one another they may trade at prices far from the general equilibrium level. But exchange serves to bring their internal valuations (*MRS*s) closer together. Over time, the dispersion in *MRS*s decreases as agents increasingly encounter others with *MRS*s similar to their own. However, as described above, the processes of production and consumption make complete convergence impossible, and so some price variance persists indefinitely.

One can get significantly larger amounts of price variance by making the market "thinner." For example, when agent interactions are restricted, less trade occurs, price convergence slows, and there results a broader disribution of *MRS*s in the economy. There are a variety of ways to produce such thin markets on the sugarscape. Here we investigate the effect of agent vision on the speed of price convergence.

In the run of the model described in figures IV-3, IV-4, and IV-5, agent vision was uniformly distributed between 1 and 5. If we reduce vision to 1 across the entire agent society, then the agents will move around much less and there will be more price heterogeneity. This is depicted in figure IV-7 where the annual mean price is displayed.

The average price over the roughly 100,000 trades that occur during this period is 1.0, quite close to the general equilibrium level. But nothing like the "law of one price" obtains. This is displayed more clearly by a plot of the standard deviation in the natural logarithm of per period mean prices (see figure IV-8). While the standard deviation trends downward, there is significantly more variation in the price than encountered in figure IV-5. In short, nothing like general equilibrium obtains here.

Price variance is a feature of real-world markets. The amount of price dispersion in any particular market is, of course, an empirical question. While we do not purport to be modeling any particular market here, the degree of price heterogeneity displayed in figure IV-8 is of the same magnitude as that observed in econometric studies of price dispersion.[38]

What matters is the equilibrum that the economy will reach from given initial conditions, not the equilibrium that it would have been in, given initial endowments, had the prices happened to be just right." See also Negishi [1961] and Hicks [1946: 127–29].

38. These include Carlson and Pescatrice [1980] and Pratt, Wise, and Zeckhauser [1979]. Economists seek to explain persistent price dispersion in terms of imperfectly

Figure IV-7. Typical Time Series for Average Trade Price under Rule System ({**G₁**}, {**M**, **T**}), with Agent Vision Set at 1

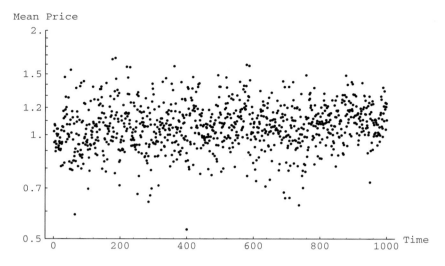

Figure IV-8. Typical Time Series for the Standard Deviation in the Logarithm of Average Trade Price under Rule System ({**G₁**}, {**M**, **T**}), with Agent Vision set at 1

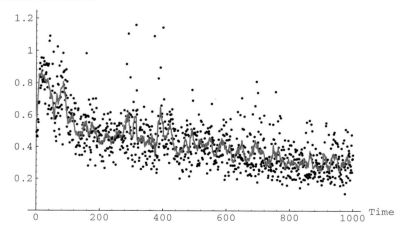

Figure IV-9. Typical Time Series for the Standard Deviation in the Logarithm of Average Trade Price under Rule System ($\{\mathbf{G_1}\}$, $\{\mathbf{M, T}\}$), with Agent Vision Uniformly Distributed between 1 and 15

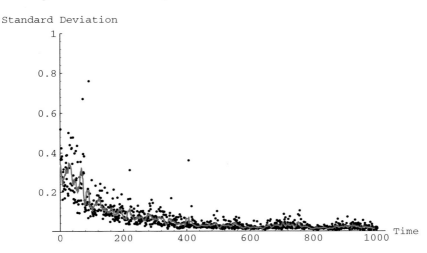

It is also possible to create markets on the sugarscape that have much *less* price variance than that shown in figure IV-5. When average agent vision is *large*, price heterogeneity *decreases*. Figure IV-9 gives a time series for the standard deviation in the logarithm of mean prices in a population in which vision is uniformly distributed between 1 and 15.

Here, due to higher mean vision, there is much more intense interaction—more perfect mixing—of the agent population and therefore equilibrium is approached quickly. By contrast to the preceding case (low agent vison, high price variance), the artificial market of figure IV-9 more closely resembles the information-rich environment of, for example, financial markets.

Non-Neoclassical Agents and Further Departures from Equilibrium

Up to now our agents, endowed with fixed preferences and infinite lives, have been basically neoclassical. In agent-based models like Sugarscape it is not difficult to relax these assumptions. In what follows we make

informed consumers who engage in (costly) search for the best prices [Ioannides 1975, Reinganum 1979]. Our model is not a search model, yet it also yields price dispersion.

our agents more human, first, by giving them finite lives and, second, by permitting their preferences to evolve. We shall see that the effect of these new rules is to add variance to the distribution of prices and to modify the price itself. In fact, the mean price will follow a kind of "random walk."

Finite Lives: Replacement

In Chapter II we introduced finite death ages into the agent population for purposes of studying the wealth distributions that emerged under rule **M**. The replacement rule $R_{[a,b]}$ denotes that the maximum agent age is uniformly distributed over interval [a,b].

In the context of trade, the effect of the replacement rule is to add agents to the population who initially have random internal valuations, that is, *MRS*s quite distant from the price levels that prevail. A new agent is born into the world with an initial endowment uncorrelated with its wants. It seeks, through trade, to improve its welfare by bringing its endowments into line with its needs. That is, an agent with high sugar metabolism and low spice metabolism wants to accumulate much larger stocks of sugar than of spice. When agent lifetimes are relatively short in comparison with the time required for the distribution of *MRS*s to homogenize, high price variance will result. An example of this is illustrated in figure IV-10, a plot of the standard deviation in the logarithm of annual average trade prices in the case of maximum age distributed uniformly between 60 and 100, and vision returned to its earlier distribution (uniform between 1 and 5). Clearly, this straightforward departure from the neoclassical agent produces market performance at considerable variance with Walrasian general equilibrium.[39]

As the average agent lifetime grows there is more time for young agents to have their internal valuations brought into line with the overall market.[40] So the price dispersion decreases as mean agent lifetime increases. This effect is shown in figure IV-11 where agent maximum ages are distributed uniformly between 980 and 1020.[41]

---

39. At any instant in this finitely lived agent economy it is certainly the case that equilibria *exist*. Figure IV-10 demonstrates that such equilibria will not generally be *achieved*.

40 One might argue that in the real world the issue is not agent lifetimes per se, but rather the duration of agents' participation in markets. Of course, in Sugarscape all agents who are alive participate in the market through rule **T**.

41. Note that the variance in agent lifetimes is identical in figures IV-10 and IV-11.

Figure IV-10. Typical Time Series for the Standard Deviation in the Logarithm of Average Trade Price under Rule System ($\{\mathbf{G}_1\}$, $\{\mathbf{M}$, $\mathbf{R}_{[60,100]}$, $\mathbf{T}\}$)

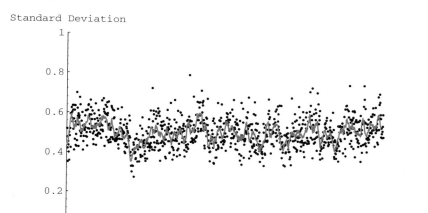

Figure IV-11. Typical Time Series for the Standard Deviation in the Logarithm of Average Trade Price under Rule System ($\{\mathbf{G}_1\}$, $\{\mathbf{M}$, $\mathbf{R}_{[960,1000]}$, $\mathbf{T}\}$)

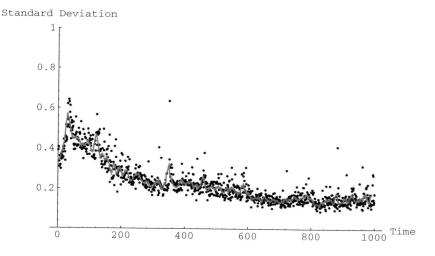

Figure IV-12. Dependence of the Long-Run Standard Deviation in the Logarithm of Average Trade Price on Average Lifetime under Rule System ($\{\mathbf{G}_1\}$, $\{\mathbf{M}, \mathbf{R}_{[a,b]}, \mathbf{T}\}$)

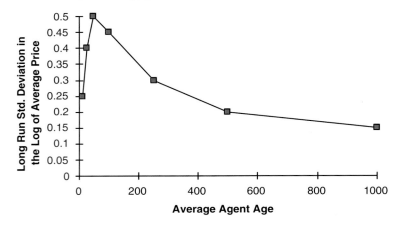

We have studied this effect for a variety of agent lifetime specifications and summarize the results in figure IV-12.

Equity

In Chapter II, highly skewed distributions of wealth were observed for agents following movement rule **M**. How is the *distribution* of wealth altered by trade? In particular, is society made more or less equitable by trade? Now that finite lives and agent replacement have been reintroduced this question is conveniently studied.[42] One familiar measure of equity is the Gini coefficient, G, illustrated in animations II-4 and III-4, where it was displayed along with Lorenz curves. In figure IV-13 the dependence of G on trade is displayed.

Overall, the effect of trade is to *further skew* the distribution of wealth in society. So, while trade increases the carrying capacity, allowing more agents to survive, it also increases the inequality of the wealth distribution. In this sense, there is a tradeoff between economic equality and economic performance.

---

42. It is not possible to study wealth distributions in the context of infinitely lived agents since such distributions are nonstationary.

Figure IV-13. Dependence of the Gini Coefficient on Trade, Parameterized by Mean Vision and Mean Metabolism, under Rule System $(\{\mathbf{G}_1\}, \{\mathbf{M}, \mathbf{R}_{[60,100]}, \mathbf{T}\})$

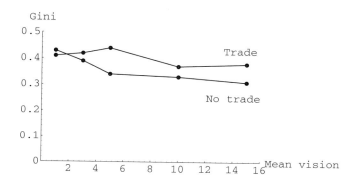

Finite Lives: Sexual Reproduction

When agents reproduce sexually via rule **S**, described in Chapter III, each new agent's preferences are the result of "cross-over" of its parents' preferences. With **S** turned on we expect—as in the case of agent replacement through $\mathbf{R}_{[a,b]}$—an increase in the price variance due to the continual introduction of novel agents (with random internal valuations) into the society. In figure IV-14 the onset of puberty is a random variable in the interval [12, 15], the range of ages at which childbearing ends is [35, 45] for women and [45, 55] for men, and the maximum agent age is selected from [60,100].

Again, a persistent high level of price dispersion is observed. Overall, the effect of finite lives—with replacement or sexual reproduction—is to push the market away from anything like general equilibrium.

As shown in Chapter III, evolutionary processes are at work whenever the agents engage in sexual reproduction, modifying the distribution of vision and metabolism in the agent population. Therefore economic preferences are systematically varying on evolutionary time scales when **S** is operational. This is so since the distributions of metabolisms in the agent population are changing, as in figure III-2, and these metabolisms enter directly into the agent welfare functions. This is a kind of "vertical transmission" of preferences. We now consider the "horizontal transmission" of preferences.

Figure IV-14. Typical Time Series for the Standard Deviation in the Logarithm of Average Trade Price under Rule System ($\{\mathbf{G}_1\}$, $\{\mathbf{M}, \mathbf{S}, \mathbf{T}\}$)

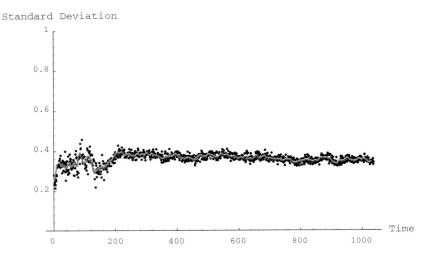

Effect of Culturally Varying Preferences

It is usual in neoclassical economics to assume fixed, exogenously given, agent preferences. The preferences of our agents, as manifested in the welfare function, although state-dependent, are fixed in the sense of being dependent on each agent's unchanging biological needs (metabolisms). It seems clear that, in fact, preferences do evolve over the course of an agent's life, as a function of contacts with other agents.[43] Imagine that the only foods are peanuts and sushi. Though born into a family of pure peanut eaters in Georgia, one might acquire a taste for sushi on a trip to Japan.

Here we let economic preferences vary according to the state of an agent's cultural tags.[44] By making agents' preferences depend on cultural variables, welfare functions evolve endogenously. In particular, call f the fraction of an agent's tags that are 0s; then $(1 - f)$ is the fraction of 1s.[45] We let these enter the welfare function according to

---

43. There is a large literature on preference formation and change, including Peleg and Yaari [1973], Stigler and Becker [1977], Cowen [1989, 1993], Karni and Schmeidler [1989], and Goodin [1990].

44. The cultural interchange machinery was introduced in Chapter III.

45. Note that the definition of group membership given in Chapter III can be stated as follows: if $f < 1/2$ then the agent belongs to the Red tribe; if $f > 1/2$, the Blue tribe.

Figure IV-15. Typical Time Series for Average Trade Price under Rule System ({**G**$_1$}, {**M, K, T**})

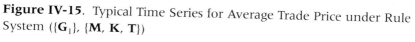

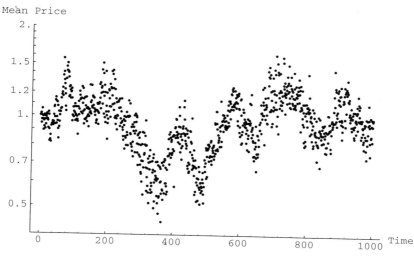

$$W(w_1, w_2) = w_1^{\frac{m_1}{\mu}f} w_2^{\frac{m_2}{\mu}(1-f)}, \tag{5}$$

where $\mu = m_1 f + m_2(1 - f)$. Thus, when cultural transmission processes are active, preferences evolve over time, yet at each instant the Cobb-Douglas algebraic form is preserved.[46]

Figure IV-15 gives a typical annual average price time series when infinitely lived agents are governed by (5) and cultural transmission rule **K** is operational.

Note that now the mean price follows a kind of random walk. This occurs because culture is continuously evolving and therefore preferences are constantly changing.[47] There is also significant price dispersion, as shown in figure IV-16.

Note that the variance in price never settles down. Also, at 10^6 transactions, the volume of trade in this run is larger (by a factor of roughly 5)

---

46. For another use of binary strings to model evolving preferences, see Lindgren and Nordahl [1994: 93–94].

47. Note that through culturally varying preferences, an agent's biological (metabolic) requirements can be eclipsed by cultural forces. For example, in the case of f near 0, an agent virtually neglects its need for sugar and, unless f increases later, the agent may die from sugar starvation.

Figure IV-16. Typical Time Series for the Standard Deviation in the Logarithm of Average Trade Price under Rule System ($\{G_1\}$, $\{M, K, T\}$)

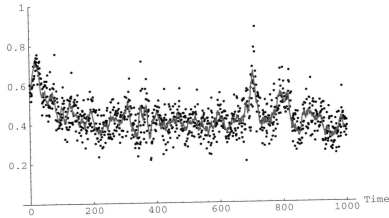

than in figure IV-4. This is because as an agent's preferences change it finds itself holding goods that it no longer values highly. Or, as Shakespeare's Benedick asks, ". . . but doth not the appetite alter? A man loves the meat in his youth that he cannot endure in his age."[48]

Let us now turn sexual reproduction (**S**) on as well, so that preferences change both "vertically" and "horizontally." A typical time series for the price standard deviation is shown in figure IV-17.

The combined effect of finite lives and evolving preferences is to produce so much variation in price that equilibrium seems lost forever.

In summary, our quite realistic departures from the neoclassical model of individual behavior produce dramatic departures from the textbook picture of overall market performance. Now we turn to another topic, restoring the neoclassical assumptions.

Externalities and Price Disequilibrium: The Effect of Pollution

In Chapter II we introduced pollution onto the sugarscape. There we were concerned with the effect of pollution on agent movement. When we turned pollution on and allowed it to accumulate (no diffusion), agents

---

48. From *Much Ado About Nothing*, Act II, Scene III.

Figure IV-17. Typical Time Series for the Standard Deviation in the Logarithm of Average Trade Price under Rule System $(\{\mathbf{G}_1\}, \{\mathbf{M}, \mathbf{S}, \mathbf{K}, \mathbf{T}\})$

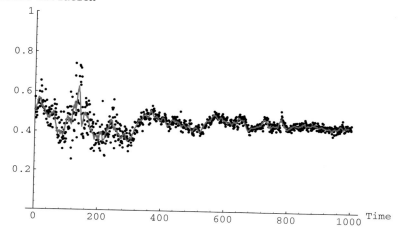

migrated from the polluted area. When we turned diffusion on, the pollution dissipated and agents moved back into the abandoned zones.

Having developed a model of bilateral trade in this chapter, we are now in a position to explore the effect of pollution on prices. To economists, environmental pollution is the classic negative externality. Externalities are important since their existence is an indication that an economy is not achieving efficient resource allocation.

To explore the effect of pollution on prices we let *one* resource, sugar, be a "dirty" good. That is, when agents harvest sugar from the landscape they leave behind production pollution. When they metabolize sugar they produce consumption pollution. Spice harvesting and consumption, by contrast, do not cause such pollution. Our experiment, then, is this. First, we will allow agents to trade. Then, after 100 periods, the agents begin generating sugar pollution and we track the effect on prices. At $t = 150$, pollution is turned off and diffusion processes are activated. Results of the experiment are logged in animation IV-3.

When the agents flee the polluted sugar mountains and move to the spice rich (sugar poor) regions, most of the sugar available to meet metabolic needs is what the fleeing agents have carried with them. Agents who need sugar must trade for it, and the relative sugar scarcity that

Animation IV-3. Price and Price Range Time Series for Pollution Accompanying Sugar Extraction and Consumption; Rule System ({**G**₁, **D**₁}, {**M**, **T**, **P**})

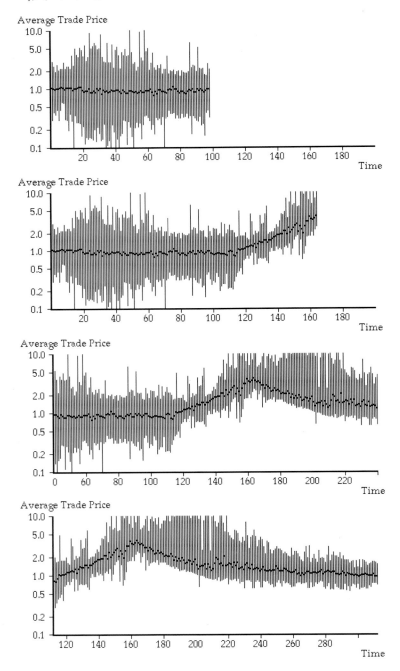

results causes the sugar price to rise.[49] The effect is dramatic, effectively an exponential price rise.

Then, when pollution generation is turned off—imagine this being the result of some technological windfall—and pollution levels are transported across the landscape by diffusion, the agents return to the sugar rich zones and the sugar price falls to its previous value of around 1.0. Such price adjustment dynamics are ignored in static microeconomics, where the implicit presumption is that, as a policy matter, it is safe to assume instant adjustment to a new equilibrium. For $t > 150$, we do indeed see adjustment back toward the original equilibrium. But from the perspective of agent society the process is far from instantaneous. In this case the artificial economy requires roughly twice as long to recover its statistical price equilibrium as it did to deviate from it. When transients such as this are long-lived, it makes little sense to focus all attention on equilibria. Artificial societies provide a means of studying price *dynamics*.

On the Evolution of Foresight

Against our simple agents it may be said that they are myopic temporally. A simple way to remedy this is to have them make decisions not on the basis of their current holdings but instead *as if* they were looking ahead ϕ periods. Formally, let the agents now move to maximize

$$W(w_1, w_2; \phi) = (w_1 - \phi m_1)^{m_1/m_T}(w_2 - \phi m_2)^{m_2/m_T}, \tag{6}$$

where the parenthesized terms on the right hand side are set equal to zero if they evaluate to a negative number.

To study how this simple kind of foresight can modify agent behavior, we initially let ϕ be uniformly distributed in the agent population in the range [0, 10], and then turn sex (that is, **S**) "on." Once more, we can "watch" evolution unfold (see figure IV-18) by tracking the average foresight in the population.

Clearly, some foresight is better than none in this society since the long-run average foresight becomes approximately stable at a nonzero level. However, large amounts of foresight, which lead agents to take actions as if they had no accumulation, are less "fit" than modest amounts.

49. Recall that prices are ratios of spice-to-sugar: A sugar price of 5 means that a buyer of sugar would sacrifice 5 units of spice to acquire 1 unit of sugar.

Figure IV-18. Evolution of Mean Foresight under Rules ($\{\mathbf{G}_1\}$, $\{\mathbf{M}, \mathbf{S}\}$)

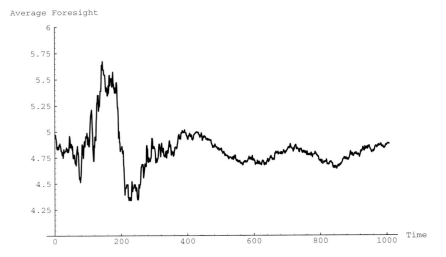

Emergent Economic Networks

Since agents in our model interact directly with each other rather than through the price system, there is a dynamic interaction structure that can be studied independent of explicit economic variables. That is, there exist well-defined networks that depict agent interactions and the evolution of such interactions.[50] Here we first describe the networks that have been implicit in the trade processes discussed above, networks of trade partners. Then we introduce a new relationship between agents, a credit rule, and study the network of lenders and borrowers that emerges.

Commodity Flows through Networks of Trade Partners

In this chapter we have specified rules for local trade between heterogeneous agents and have studied the markets that emerged. All trade was between neighboring agents. There thus exists a network of trade partners.[51] To depict such a network, let each agent be a node of a graph and

---

50. Other models of trade networks include Kauffman [1988] and Tesfatsion [1995].

51. Since all trade partners are neighbors, but not conversely, the trade partner network is a subgraph of the neighborhood network, defined in Chapter II.

draw edges between agents who are trade partners. Such trade networks are endogenous in that they depend in a complicated way on agent behavior (that is, the movement rule, trade rule, and so on). They change over time, of course, as agents move around the landscape. Animation IV-4 gives such an evolution.

It is useful to think of the edges in such networks as channels over which commodities flow.[52] Notice that although any particular agent trades with at most 4 neighbors, agents who are quite distant spatially may be part of the same graph, that is, connected economically. In essence, such graphs portray large-scale flows of goods across the landscape.[53]

Credit Networks and the Emergence of Hierarchy

So far the agent societies studied in this book have been "flat"—there is no sense in which some agents are subordinate to others. This stems from the fact that agent interactions are usually short lived, lasting one (or at most a few) periods, or are symmetrical (such as when agents are neighbors of one another, or are mutual friends).

We can produce *hierarchical* relationships among agents by permitting them to borrow from and lend to one another for purposes of having children. The following local rule of credit produces such relationships:[54]

> Agent credit rule $\mathbf{L}_{dr}$:
> - An agent is a *potential lender* if it is too old to have children, in which case *the maximum amount it may lend is one-half of its current wealth*;
> - An agent is a *potential lender* if it is *of* childbearing age and has wealth in excess of the amount necessary to have children, in which case *the maximum amount it may lend is the excess wealth*;
> - An agent is a *potential borrower* if it is of childbearing age *and* has insufficient wealth to have a child *and* has income (resources gathered, minus metabolism, minus other loan obligations) in the present period making it credit-worthy for a loan written at terms specified by the lender;

---

52. As in Chapter III, lines across the entire lattice connect trade partners who are neighbors on the torus.

53. For why this network does not have a pure von Neumann structure, see footnote 29 in Chapter II.

54. Insofar as a primary consequence of this rule is that older agents lend to younger ones, a kind of finely grained overlapping generations model results.

Animation IV-4. Emergent Trade Network under Rule System ($\{\mathbf{G}_1\}$, $\{\mathbf{M}, \mathbf{T}\}$)

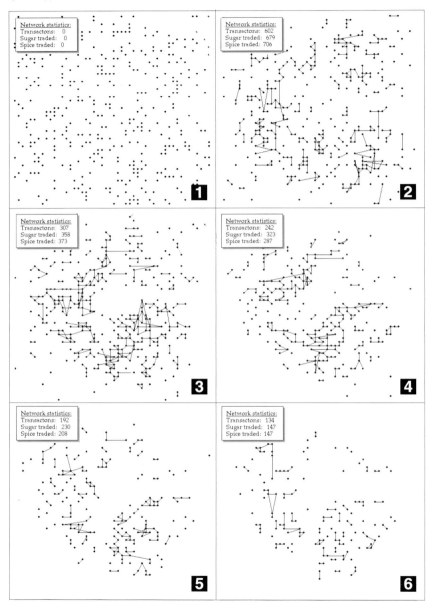

- If a potential borrower and a potential lender are neighbors then a loan is originated with a duration of d years at the rate of r percent, and the face value of the loan amount is transferred from the lender to the borrower;
- At the time of the loan due date, if the borrower has sufficient wealth to repay the loan then a transfer from the borrower to the lender is made; else the borrower is required to pay back half of its wealth and a new loan is originated for the remaining sum;
- If the borrower on an active loan dies before the due date then the lender simply takes a loss;
- If the lender on an active loan dies before the due date then the borrower is not required to pay back the loan, unless inheritance rule **I** is active, in which case the lender's children now become the borrower's creditors.

This rule may not seem at first glance to be particularly parsimonious. However, it is the simplest one we could think of that bore some resemblance to real-world credit arrangements.

We return to the one commodity landscape to illustrate the operation of this rule. When agents move, engage in sexual activity, and borrow from and lend to one another, there result credit relationships like those shown in animation IV-5.[55] This animation begins by displaying agents spatially, coloring lenders green, borrowers red, and yellow those agents who are both borrowers and lenders. Subsequently, the hierarchical evolution is displayed. Agents at the top of the hierarchical plot are pure lenders, those at the bottom of any branch are pure borrowers, and agents in between are simultaneously borrowers and lenders. For this run as many as five levels of lenders-borrowers emerge.

Social Computation, Emergent Computation

The theory of general equilibrium is essentially a body of results on the *existence* of equilibrium. In the neoclassical story, the Walrasian auctioneer is a *mechanism* for achieving such an equilibrium. Once the market-clearing price is determined, the population of price-taking agents

---

55. The Sugarscape software system implements the n commodity generalization of credit rule **L**. For the sake of simplicity, the single commodity (sugar-only) form is used here.

Animation IV-5. Emergent Credit Network under Rule System ($\{\mathbf{G}_1\}$, $\{\mathbf{M}, \mathbf{S}, \mathbf{L}_{10,10}\}$)

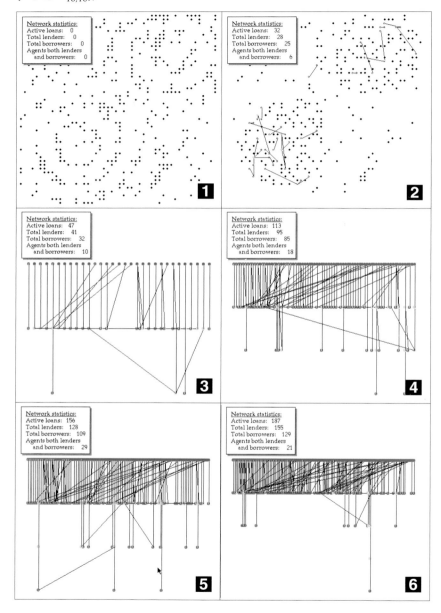

produces a socially optimal allocation of goods through exchange. The auctioneer is essentially an *algorithm* for the computation of prices. In this picture of the economic world no single agent has enough information (about endowments, preferences) to compute an efficient allocation on its own. Yet this allocation results through the cumulative actions of individuals. However, a particularly curious characteristic of this picture of decentralized decisionmaking via prices is that the auctioneer algorithm requires *centralized* information. That is, all agents must report their demands to the auctioneer who ultimately furnishes an authoritative price to the population that all agents *must* use in their trade decisions.

In reality, of course, there is no auctioneer, no *central price computation authority*. Rather, prices emerge from the interactions of agents. These interactions occur in parallel and asynchronously. It is *as if* agents are processing nodes in some large-scale parallel, asynchronous computer. Trade is the algorithm the nodes execute; nodes communicate prices to one another and change their internal states through the exchange of goods. The computation topology (architecture) is endogenous and ever-changing. Under what circumstances do such computations terminate in a market-clearing price? And how would any particular agent know that they had terminated—is it even possible to discern whether an equilibrium price has been achieved?[56] Does the fact that some nodes die while new nodes are regularly added to the social computer mean that notions of computation termination must be stochastic in nature?

Insofar as real economic agents engage in trade to improve their welfare, one might view the parallel, asynchronous exchange activities of agents not as the social computation of prices but as a distributed algorithm for the production of agent welfare. Artificial economies are laboratories where we can study the relative performance of distinct trade rules (algorithms) and alternative computational architectures (agent networks) in producing agent welfare.

Social computation concerns how societies of interacting agents solve problems that agents alone cannot solve, or even pose. Emergent computation concerns how networks of interacting computational nodes solve problems that nodes alone cannot solve.[57] Notice that these two fields have much in common.

---

56. Technically, these questions are very complicated. In the context of parallel, asynchronous computation, the relevant literature concerns the snapshot algorithm; see Bertsekas and Tsitsiklis [1989: 579–87].

57. For more on emergent computation, see Forrest [1991].

Summary and Conclusions

In many ways, the central question of economic theory is this: To what extent can economic markets efficiently allocate goods and services among agents? For example, does the ostensibly good performance of markets like stock exchanges tell us anything about the functioning of decentralized markets such as those for environmental goods and services? In our model we have just such a decentralized market—decentralized spatially—and we have found mixed results, to say the least, concerning the achievability of equilibrium prices and globally optimal allocations, under a wide variety of conditions.

Policy Implications

Foley [1994] has thoroughly criticized the way in which conclusions about economic policy are drawn from the model of Walrasian competitive equilibrium. In particular, the orthodox criticism of price regulation is that it is *irrelevant* if prices already fall within the limits set by the regulations or *distorting* if it actually constrains price movements. But in decentralized markets there is no single price.

> If a significant amount of trading takes place at different price ratios, price floors and ceilings can serve to protect agents against relatively disadvantageous trades, and thus to mitigate the endogenous horizontal inequality produced by the market. [Foley 1994: 342]

Therefore, a clear role for economic regulation may exist when prices are heterogeneous.

Certain economists ascribe nearly magical powers to markets. Markets are idealized to operate frictionlessly, without central authority, costlessly allocating resources to their most efficient use. In this world of complete decentralization and Pareto efficiency, the only possible effect of government intervention is to "gum up" the perfect machinery. While this extreme view is perhaps little more than a caricature—and few would admit to holding it in toto—it is also, unfortunately, a position frequently promulgated in policy circles, especially when there is no econometric or other evidence upon which to base decisionmaking.[58]

A different way to frame the issues raised in this chapter is as follows:

---

58. On the limited extent to which economic theory provides solid foundations for policy, see Hahn [1981] and Kirman [1989].

Do plausible departures from the axioms of general equilibrium theory produce markets that behave almost as well as ideal markets? While few would admit that extant markets function ideally, there is little cogent theory of performance degradation in real markets resulting from incomplete information, imperfect foresight, finite lives, evolving preferences, or external economies, for example.

The emphasis in the economics literature has been on the *existence* of static equilibrium, without any explicit microdynamics. Why cannot prices oscillate periodically on seasonal or diurnal time scales, or quasi-periodically when subject to shocks, or even chaotically?[59] Is it not reasonable to expect generational or other long-term structural shifts in the economy to produce prices that follow a trend as opposed to staying constant? Might not far from equilibrium behavior be a more reasonable description of a real economy?[60] From the computational evidence above, we think that there is good reason to be skeptical of the predominant focus on fixed-point equilibria. Economies of autonomous adaptive agents—and of humans—may be far from equilibrium systems. And, in turn, far from equilibrium economics might well turn out to be far richer than equilibrium economics.

---

59. Indeed, there is a growing *theoretical* literature that admits these possibilities; see, for example, Bala and Majumdar [1992]. However, these results do not seem to have made their way into policy discussions as of this writing.

60. As Farmer has observed, "To someone schooled in nonlinear dynamics, economic time series look very far from equilibrium, and the emphasis of economic theories on equilibria seems rather bizarre. In fact, the use of the word equilibrium in economics appears to be much closer to the notion of attractor as it is used in dynamics rather than any notion of equilibrium used in physics" [Anderson, Arrow, and Pines 1988: 101].

V

Disease Processes

Immunology concerns the dynamics of infection *within* an individual. Epidemiology concerns the spread of infections *between* individuals, and hence through populations. While the two are obviously related, there is little in the way of unified theory. Immunology is one field, epidemiology another. Moreover, as in demography—discussed in Chapter III—the models that do exist in these fields are essentially "top down," involving highly aggregate, low dimensional systems of differential equations. In this chapter we offer *a unified bottom-up immunology-epidemiology model* and discuss how the intra- and interagent infection dynamics may interact with other social processes, such as migration and trade.

Models of Disease Transmission and Immune Response

To model the spread of infectious diseases through a population, mainstream mathematical epidemiology divides the population into subgroups, compartments such as "susceptibles," "infectives," and "removeds" (for example, quarantined), and then posits various differential equations tracking the flow of individuals from one pool to the next.[1] The Kermack-McKendrick [Murray 1989: 612] equations exemplify this ordinary differential equations (ODE) approach. In that well-known model, susceptibles contract the disease (that is, become infective) through contacts with infectives; infectives are removed from circulation at some rate proportional to their numbers.[2] In this case, the flow is from susceptible to infective to removed; for that reason, it is termed an S-I-R model. Such models have the important property of being mathematically tractable—at least there is a large arsenal of

---

1. Sometimes finite difference equations are used instead of differential equations. The thrust of our critique is not affected by this distinction.

2. Technically, one distinguishes between the pathogen—a microparasite, for instance—and the disease, as a set of symptoms. For modeling purposes, we ignore the distinction.

analytical and numerical tools that can be brought to bear on them. The approach, moreover, has fundamentally illuminated, for example, the threshold nature of epidemics and has elegantly explained such counterintuitive phenomena as herd immunity,[3] both of which have important implications for public health policies. The younger field of mathematical immunology is yielding the same kinds of important qualitative insights.[4]

Heterogeneous People, Homogeneous Models

These strengths, however, come at an expense in realism. In Kermack-McKendrick type models, for example, "if you've seen one susceptible, you've seen 'em all." That is, these models are highly aggregate. There is simply a state variable, $S(t)$, representing the number (or fraction) of susceptibles in society at time t. A susceptible is a susceptible is a susceptible; the same goes for infectives, $I(t)$, and so on. Agents, in short, are *homogeneous*.[5] In reality, of course, agents are *heterogeneous* precisely in that they have different immune systems.[6]

In our model, every agent is born with a distinct immune system, capable of adaptation to ward off disease. Immune systems are genetically transmitted from parents at birth and are distinguished from either parent's immune *phenotype*. This genotype-phenotype distinction is discussed below, where the precise immune system that is inherited from the parents is described in detail. Agent immune systems "try" (in a precise sense to be explained) to "code for" parasites as these are passed from agent to agent.[7] This brings us to our treatment of space.

---

3. In a well-mixed population—a herd—if some initial fraction is immunized then the disease cannot survive in the herd. In this sense, the herd enjoys immunity though not all members of the herd do; see Edelstein-Keshet [1988: 254].

4. Perelson [1989] offers a lucid introduction to theoretical immunology.

5. More elaborate models disaggregate further, defining sub-types within the susceptible (or infective) pool, $S_i(t)$, for $i = 1,..., n$. But, for each i, the group is homogeneous. Of course, when n equals the size of the total population, one has, in effect, an agent-based model.

6. Attempts to formally model heterogeneous populations—for instance, Nold [1980], May and Anderson [1984], and Boylan [1991]—show the importance of heterogeneity, but very quickly lead to intractable mathematics and recourse to traditional computer simulation. Even the addition of seemingly innocuous features like nonconstant population to standard models can yield formidably complicated nonlinear dynamical systems (for example, Busenberg and van den Driessche [1990], Derrick and van den Driessche [1993], and Gao and Hethcote [1992]).

7. We have consistently used the term "agent" to denote individual humans, and we continue this usage in the present chapter. However, to avoid confusion, it is worth

Separate Space

In ODE models, there is no space whatever; society is modeled as a well-stirred chemical reactor. Partial differential equation models, for example, reaction-diffusion systems, couple these *reaction* kinetics to some sort of spatial process, such as *diffusion*. In such models the agent society is treated as a continuous function of space. Diseases propagate—as, for instance, traveling waves—across agent society, idealized as a continuous medium.[8]

In our artificial society—and in the real world—agents are completely distinct from the space they inhabit. When diseases occur in our model they are, to be sure, passed from agent to agent (depending on individual immunity), but the environment, the sugarscape—and the agents' rules for interaction with it—shapes the spatial distribution of agents, and hence shapes the epidemic dynamics. In Sugarscape, agents might come into contact while searching for sugar, and so the (ever-changing) topography of the sugarscape affects the epidemic dynamics. In turn, events that produce migrations—like sudden environmental changes—have the effect of forcing separate disease pools together, thereby confronting immune systems with new infections, allowing us to "grow" scenarios of the sort recounted colorfully by William McNeill in his book *Plagues and Peoples* [1976]. We will return to these "proto-epidemics" once the model has been described.

Immune System Response

Before presenting our model in detail, it should be emphasized that the human immune system is a fantastically complex apparatus whose primary functions include:

- recognizing parasites, bacteria, and viruses;
- mounting defenses that are highly specific to the invaders in question;
- remembering the foreign invaders' structures, and maintaining a capability to defend against subsequent attacks.[9]

---

noting that traditional epidemiology uses the term "host" where we use "agent," and "infectious agent" where we use "disease."

8. See Murray [1989: 651–95] for deterministic models; Oelschläger [1992] develops a stochastic model.

9. Typical curves for serum antibodies over time show the secondary response as both faster and stronger (that is, generating more defender cells, namely lymphocytes) than the primary reaction.

The actual mechanisms whereby the human immune system accomplishes these diverse tasks are far from completely understood.

In modeling the immune system, differential equations have been the primary tool. Here we develop a bottom-up model, of which many are possible. One agent-based approach would be to let microparasites (the diseases) "graze" on human society, just as agents graze the sugarscape—the parasites would then constitute a second population of agents. Meanwhile, inside each agent host, there would be a detailed immune system model.[10] However, this approach would be computationally daunting. We develop a simpler—but, we believe, novel and illuminating—bottom-up model.

As always in this work, our goal is to devise simple local rules under which the phenomena of interest emerge. Some of what emerges below—immune learning and memory—is internal to the agents. Other emergent phenomena—epidemics that spread across the sugarscape—are external. We will work with strings of 0s and 1s, using a formalism akin to that employed earlier to study cultural processes. First, we describe how an inherited immune system learns and remembers. Later, we explain exactly what immune system each child inherits from its parents.

Binary Strings

To begin, every agent is born with an "immune system" consisting of a string of 0s and 1s, a *binary string*. A "disease" is also a string of 0s and 1s. Diseases may be of different lengths but are always shorter than immune systems.

A graphical, or "shape space," interpretation of these strings is natural. Immune systems and diseases can be thought of as linear combinations of step functions of unit height. Immune system 0011101011 is depicted in figure V-1. In our model, immune response is simply the process whereby the immune system attempts to "deform" itself locally to match each disease it encounters.

So, imagine a disease, D = 10011. What happens when an individual immune system is confronted with disease D? Since the immune sys-

---

10. By a detailed model we mean one that explicitly represents such immune system functions as lymphocyte proliferation and antibody development. For detailed immune system models, see Perelson [1988].

Figure V-1. Shape-Space Interpretation of Binary String 0011101011

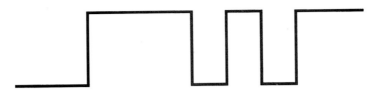

tem is simply a longer sequence of 0s and 1s, either disease D is a sub-string of the immune system or it is not. If it is, then the agent is immune to the disease. If no substring of the immune system matches the disease, then the agent searches its immune system for the substring closest to D—the substring disagreeing with D in the fewest bit positions. Recall from the discussion of cultural tags in Chapter III that the number of bitwise disagreements between two strings is the Hamming distance between them. So, the immune system—call it I—searches itself for the substring closest to D in Hamming distance. If there is more than one such substring, the first one encountered in moving (along I) from left to right is chosen.[11] Then, each time period, a bit on that "nearest" substring of I is flipped to agree with D, until D is matched (at which point the agent is immune). Now, suppose this process of "learning," or "coding for" D, takes 5 periods. During that time, the agent is infected with D, it can pass D to neighbors, and, importantly, its metabolism is increased by some amount.

Symptoms

This metabolic "fee" is plausible from the point of view of both parasite and host. Viruses, for example, enter hosts precisely because "they lack the necessary machinery to manufacture proteins and *metabolize* sugars."[12] So, in letting our digital diseases "steal" metabolic capacity from their hosts we are treating them literally as parasites. The imposition of some metabolic fee also makes qualitative sense from the host's perspective. Fevers are literally increases in caloric expenditure—our bodies heat up when we are sick.

---

11. That is, the leftmost substring is selected.
12. Anderson and May [1991: 27].

There may be further manifestations of a disease. For example, we could easily reduce the agent's vision while it is infected. Or, we could interrupt its normal sexual activity. Different diseases can have different effects. The essential point, however, is that there normally *are* effects. This raises another criticism of standard "top-down" epidemic models: There is no recognizable difference in the *behavior* of infected agents. From the equations themselves, that is, there would be no reason to suspect that having the disease was in any way undesirable or incapacitating; uniform mixing continues; transmission kinetics are unaffected. In our model, the metabolic fee immediately alters the agent's behavior. Recall that movement and trading behavior depend on the agent's utility function, which depends explicitly on metabolic rates. Hence, because its metabolic rate is affected, a sick agent will *behave differently* than a healthy agent. Obviously, if, in addition to metabolism, vision is affected, behavior will be altered further. For simplicity, we include only a metabolic effect here.

In order to discuss immunological memory, multiple diseases, and certain other topics, a numerical example of immune learning will repay study. Let us walk through the single disease case.

The Immunological Response Rule

Consider a length ten immune system I = 1011101001 and, as before, let D = 10011. Note that D does not match any substring of I. So an agent with immune system I would contract D on contact with an agent suffering from it. This now sick agent's metabolism would be hiked by, say, one, and it would begin searching I for the closest match. Comparing D to the five digits of I beginning at position 1, we see disagreement at a single position (Hamming distance 1). Comparing D to the five digits of I beginning with position 2, we find a Hamming distance of 4, and so on, as shown in table V-1.

From this table we see that the first 5 bits of I (start position 1) is the substring that best matches D. Since the immune system is only off by 1 bit (at I's position 3), learning D takes only 1 period. For that cycle, the agent's metabolism is hiked by one and the agent can pass the disease to neighbors. After having "coded for" disease D, the immune system is transformed into 1001101001.

Table V-1. Initial Mismatch between the Immune System
1011101001 and Disease 10011

Start position	Immune system										Hamming distance
	1	0	1	1	1	0	1	0	0	1	
1	1	0	0	1	1						1
2		1	0	0	1	1					4
3			1	0	0	1	1				3
4				1	0	0	1	1			2
5					1	0	0	1	1		3
6						1	0	0	1	1	3

Immunological Memory as Lock-In

If nothing happens to alter the first five bits of this trained immune system, then the agent will be permanently immune to disease D. In short, the trained immune system, having "coded for" D, will *remember* it.[13] The important phenomenon of immunological memory arises very naturally from our simple model, in much the same way that "lock-in" arises in other fields.[14]

Having worked a numerical example, we now state the general immune response rule. When a disease confronts an immune system the rule applied each time period is as follows:

Agent immune response rule:
- If the disease is a substring of the immune system then end (the agent is immune), else (the agent is infected) go to the following step;
- The substring in the agent immune system having the smallest Hamming distance from the disease is selected and the first bit at which it is different from the disease string is changed to match the disease.

---

13. For attempts to capture immunological memory with differential equations, see Anderson and May [1991: 32–35].

14. For discussions of "lock-in," see Arthur [1988, 1990].

Disease Transmission

Having discussed immune response to disease, we now turn to inter-agent disease transmission. In reality, humans may contract diseases through contact with other people or with disease vectors (such as insects or animals). Given that there is only one class of agents on the sugarscape, we have no ability to model the latter mode of contact. Therefore, diseases are transmitted between neighboring agents. The disease transmission rule, observed by all agents who are infected with at least one disease, is as follows:

> <u>Agent disease transmission rule</u>: For each neighbor, a disease that currently afflicts the agent is selected at random and given to the neighbor.

We model disease processes with the immune response and disease transmission rules given above, and we will always use them together. Hence, for notational compactness, denote their combined application by **E**.

Multiple Diseases

At any time there may be many diseases in circulation, a situation easi-ly handled in our model. Suppose an agent with three diseases has moved next to you. One of its diseases is selected at random for trans-mission to you. The immune response rule described above is applied: If your immune system can find a matching substring then you do not contract the disease. Otherwise, your immune system finds the substring closest to the disease in Hamming space and begins flipping, during which time you suffer a metabolic fee characteristic of that disease. Each additional disease contracted imposes its characteristic metabolic penal-ty. Now, it may be that in "learning" a certain disease, the immune sys-tem "unlearns" diseases to which it has earlier become immune. So, agents may catch the same disease many times. Immunological memo-ry, in other words, can be corrupted in a world of multiple diseases. This leads to the possibility of distinct diseases enjoying "mutualistic" rela-tions. For example, no immune system of length three could simulta-neously code for the two diseases: 11 and 00. The instant the immune system matches one of them it is vulnerable to the other.

Genotypes and Phenotypes

We have discussed how, in Sugarscape, an agent's immune system, inherited at birth, learns to combat diseases. But, what immune system is actually inherited? In the course of *their* lives, an agent's parents may have acquired immunity to a variety of infectious diseases; that is, their immune systems have "trained on" and coded for these diseases. However, the child does not inherit the *trained* immune system—the mature *phenotype*—of either parent. It inherits an immune system *genotype* that is a "crossover" of the *untrained* immune genotypes of its parents, plus possibly some mutation.

For example, imagine that two agents, Adam and Eve, are born with the first two immune *genomes*—two strings of fifty random 0s and 1s. They immediately begin training on whatever diseases are floating around the Garden of Eden. While the immunocompetences (phenotypes) of both Adam and Eve are thus changing through training, their immune *genomes* are not. It is as though one *copy* of the agent's initial immune genome—a template, if you will—is immediately set aside, put on file, and held for later genetic transmission, while the second copy begins training at once and is the operative infection-fighting system of the agent. This is how it works in our simple model. Specifically, given the *untrained* immune systems of its parents, the child's *untrained* immune system is determined as follows.

At bit positions where mom's and dad's *genomes* agree, the child inherits their common value. For each bit position where mom and dad differ, the child gets either its father's or its mother's value with equal probability. This object, the genotype, is then set aside for later genetic transmission, while a *copy* of it, the phenotype, begins training upon exposure to disease.[15]

Childhood Diseases

One quite realistic result of this scheme is that, while an agent's parents may have *acquired* an immunity to a particular disease, D—that is, they have matched that pattern at the *phenotypic* level—their untrained immune *genomes* do not contain D as a substring. Hence, each genera-

---

15. The Sugarscape software system permits mutations to diseases and genotypes at user-specified rates. Hence, perpetual coevolution of diseases and immune systems can occur. In the runs of the model below these mutation rates are set to zero to keep things as simple as possible.

tion must "learn" D all over again! Indeed, this is why chicken pox persists as a childhood disease. Lamarckians—who believed in the genetic transmission of acquired attributes—would have no explanation for this phenomenon. We now see the persistence of certain childhood diseases as manifesting the gap between phenotype (the trained system) and genotype (the untrained, transmitted template).

Having reviewed the model, let us now run some cases.[16] Nature— that is to say, the computer—maintains a master list of all diseases. Each disease on the list is a random binary string, its length a random number between one and ten. We will consider two cases, first when the master list holds 10 diseases, and then 25.

Digital Diseases on the Sugarscape

With a master disease list of length 10, there are 10 possible diseases an agent might contract. Every agent is given copies of four randomly selected diseases from the list. Immune systems are binary strings of length 50.[17] Initially the 0s and 1s are assigned randomly. The rules for disease transmission *between* agents—the epidemic model—and for immune response *within* the individual—the immunological model—are both in operation. Agents are moving around the sugarscape as in Chapter II, following rule **M**. Starting the agents in random positions, and coloring the "sick" (that is, those having at least one disease) red and the "well" blue, the epidemic unfolds in animation V-1.

One can track any particular disease, but the main result of this run is that society is able to rid itself of all diseases. The next case is somewhat more challenging to the agents' immune systems.

Now we enlarge the disease master list to 25 diseases, and we initially give every agent 10 distinct, randomly drawn diseases from the list. Again coloring for healthy and sick, the dynamics are represented in animation V-2.

---

16. Throughout, agents have access to neither vaccine nor medicine. While there are no medical institutions in our bottom-up model, it is worth noting how one might use models like Sugarscape to study alternative public health policies. A medicine might be interpreted as a substance that boosts the immune system response rate each cycle. Unmedicated agents are allowed to flip one immune bit per cycle; medicated agents might be permitted 2 flips, for instance. Alternatively, medications that treat only symptoms would reduce only the metabolic "fees" imposed by diseases on agents. To model vaccination against a particular disease, one might simply append the entire disease string to a vaccinated agent's immune system, producing instant immunity to the disease.

17. Thus there are 2^{50} possible distinct immune systems.

Animation V-1. Society Rids Itself of Disease under Rules $(\{G_1\}, \{M, E\})$

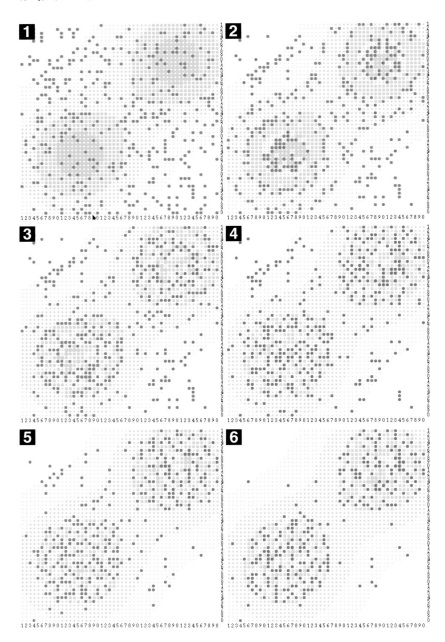

Animation V-2. Society Unable to Rid Itself of Disease under Rules $(\{\mathbf{G}_1\}, \{\mathbf{M}, \mathbf{E}\})$

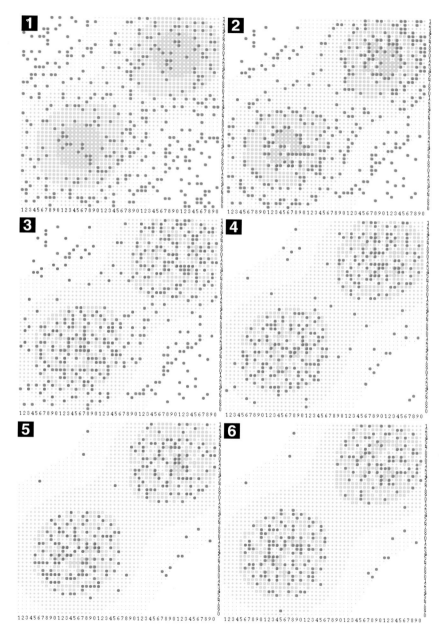

In this case, society is unable to attain universal health. An endemic level of infection is sustained.

It is noteworthy that *some* of the immune systems are doing something quite marvelous. There are certainly agents whose immune system is shorter than the *sum* of the lengths of the diseases with which they are confronted. Immune systems are of length 50 and the disease pool has *average* length 5.5 (since diseases are of random length between 1 and 10). Hence, it is likely that for some agents, their 10 diseases, laid end to end, are longer than their immune systems. Immune systems that clear themselves of these diseases thus cannot be "solving" the problem by brute force, that is, laying the diseases end to end. Rather, successful immune response involves overlaying common substrings.

Disease Transmission Networks

We kept track of neighborhood agent networks in Chapter II, of genealogical and friendship networks in Chapter III, and of trading relationships and credit in Chapter IV. If we now draw lines between sick agents and the agents from whom they contracted their sickness, a kind of disease transmission network arises.[18] A disease connection network in which society fails to rid itself of all diseases is shown in animation V-3.

Such networks are the "space" in which diseases travel. The structure of such networks defines the character of transmission dynamics. For example, networks having small diameter may be associated with a few infected agents transmitting their disease to all the other agents.[19]

Real epidemics occur in a social context. Social behaviors such as trade, migration, and conquest function to introduce new diseases into "virgin" populations, thereby confronting agent immune systems with novel challenges. An interesting possibility, therefore, is to *connect the epidemic's spatial and temporal dynamics to other social processes*, such as military expansion, migration, or trade.

Many such connections are set forth in William McNeill's fascinating book *Plagues and Peoples* [1976]. For example, McNeill recounts how, in China, bubonic plague was spread by military action:

---

18. See Wallace [1991] for a discussion of AIDS transmission networks. Rapoport and Yuan [1989] discuss epidemics from a social networks perspective.

19. The diameter of a graph is the minimum number of edges needed to connect any two nodes of the graph.

Animation V-3. Disease Transmission Network under Rules $(\{\mathbf{G}_1\}, \{\mathbf{M}, \mathbf{E}\})$

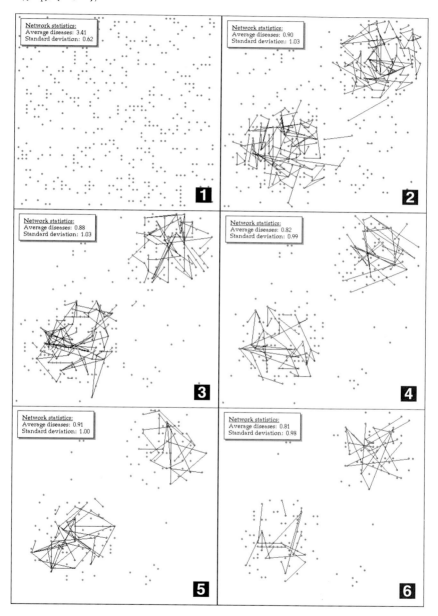

1

Network statistics:
Average diseases: 3.41
Standard deviation: 0.62

2

Network statistics:
Average diseases: 0.90
Standard deviation: 1.03

3

Network statistics:
Average diseases: 0.88
Standard deviation: 1.03

4

Network statistics:
Average diseases: 0.82
Standard deviation: 0.99

5

Network statistics:
Average diseases: 0.91
Standard deviation: 1.00

6

Network statistics:
Average diseases: 0.81
Standard deviation: 0.98

> Early in the nineteenth century, the upper reaches of the Salween River constituted the boundary between infected and uninfected areas. Then in 1855 a military revolt broke out in Yunan. Chinese troops were sent across the Salween to suppress the rebels, and, being unfamiliar with the risks of bubonic infection, contracted the disease and carried it back with them into the rest of China. Thereafter, outbreaks of plague continued to occur in various parts of the Chinese interior without attracting much attention from the outside world, until in 1894 the disease reached Canton and Hong Kong and sent a chill of fright through the European settlements in those ports. [McNeill 1976: 152]

While military intervention brought the plague to these ports, trade and technology (the steamship) account for its transmission from there:

> . . . the steamship network that arose in the 1870s was the vehicle that dispersed the infection around the globe, and did so, once the epidemic broke out in Canton and Hong Kong, with a speed that was limited only by the speed with which a ship could carry its colony of infected rats and fleas to a new port. Speed was obviously decisive in allowing a chain of infection to remain unbroken from port to port. [McNeill 1976: 156]

In the language of Chapter III's proto-history, Blue agents penetrate Red society, catch new infections, return to the Blue zone, and then Blue society experiences the epidemic. Or, in their search for "sugar," a small band of infected agents may enter a healthy society touching off the epidemic. Indeed, as McNeill recounts, even a single foreign agent can suffice.

> In 1903 a South American tribe, the Cayapo, accepted a missionary— a single priest—who bent every effort to safeguard his flock from the evils and dangers of civilization. When he arrived the tribe was between six thousand and eight thousand strong, yet only five hundred survived in 1918. By 1927 only twenty-seven percent were alive and in 1950 two or three individuals tracing descent to the Cayapo still existed, but the tribe had totally disappeared—and this despite the best intentions and a deliberate attempt to shield the Indians from disease as well as other risks of outside contacts. [McNeill 1976: 204]

Clearly, this would not be a difficult story to "grow" in our model. A healthy tribe of agents, their immune systems "tuned" to cope with a familiar pool of diseases, would suffer this fate if confronted with a sufficiently novel infection. The immune systems simply would not be able to code for the new strain before it takes a terrifying toll.

VI

Conclusions

The main point of the preceding chapters is simply this: *A wide range of important social, or collective, phenomena can be made to emerge from the spatio-temporal interaction of autonomous agents operating on landscapes under simple local rules.*

Summary

Let us review some of the main results. Using only the rule of gradient search (**M** from Chapter II) all sorts of things emerged on the sugarscape: the principle of carrying capacity, waves of agents propagating in directions unavailable to the individuals, highly skewed wealth distributions, and migratory behavior—all from the same simple local rule. Then, in Chapter III we saw that a wide range of population trajectories was produced by a simple sex rule, **S**; that culture rule **K** was sufficient to "grow" spatially segregated "tribes"; and that combat rule C_α yielded a range of conflict modes. Finally, when rules were combined, an entire proto-history unfolded on the sugarscape. By adding a second commodity in Chapter IV, we were able to grow simple markets. Results resembling general economic equilibrium were obtained using completely decentralized, bilateral trade rules, that is, without a Walrasian auctioneer. But, the near-equilibrium behavior was shown to rest heavily on neoclassical assumptions of fixed preferences and infinite lives. When the textbook assumptions were relaxed, the economy was pushed further from equilibrium. From a policy standpoint, the analysis raises deep questions as to the allocative efficiency of unregulated markets. While trade generally increases the carrying capacity of the environment, it can also increase wealth inequality; in this sense, there is a tradeoff between equity and efficiency. The statistical equilibria that do emerge are accompanied by horizontal inequality, vitiating the welfare theorems of general equilibrium theory. Finally, in Chapter V, we modeled the evolution of individual immune sytems, as infectious diseases were passed from agent to agent. Fundamental immunological and epidemiological phenomena such as immune memory and the persistence of childhood diseases both emerged naturally from the model. And connections between disease processes and other social phenomena, of the sort discussed by McNeill [1976], were made.

Emergent Society

Over the preceeding chapters, we have built agent rules of movement, sexual reproduction, cultural transmission, group membership, trade, inheritance, credit, immune response, and disease propagation. As a culminating run let us turn all these rules "on" at once, and see what artificial society results. It will be a society of considerable complexity, with many interacting spheres of activity. But, we have also developed scientific instruments allowing us to view various "slices" of the whole. Indeed, in animation VI-1 you will see the following, listed in the order in which they appear:[1]

1. Top-down view of agents hiving the sugarscape, colored red if diseased, blue if disease-free;
2. Social networks of neighbors;
3. Sugar wealth histogram;
4. Spice wealth histogram;
5. Lorenz curve and Gini coefficient for total wealth;
6. Population time series;
7. Age histogram;
8. Genealogical networks (family trees);
9. Cultural tag histogram;
10. Network of friends;
11. Average price time series;
12. Price standard deviation time series;
13. Trade volume time series;
14. Trade network;
15. Spatial credit network;
16. Hierarchical credit network;
17. Disease time series;
18. Disease transmission network.

---

1. Users of the CD-ROM will get a flavor of the Sugarscape software system as a "virtual user" selects various menu items.

Animation VI-1. Evolution of an Artificial Society under Rules ($\{\mathbf{G}_1\}$, $\{\mathbf{M}, \mathbf{S}, \mathbf{K}, \mathbf{T}, \mathbf{L}_{10,10}, \mathbf{E}\}$)

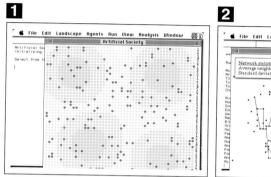

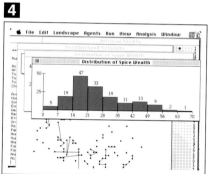

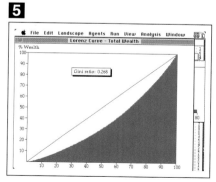

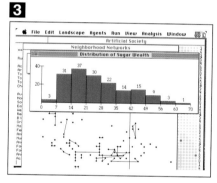

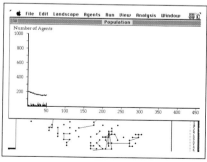

Animation VI-1. *Continued*

7

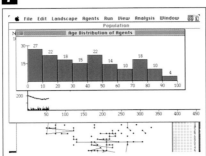

8

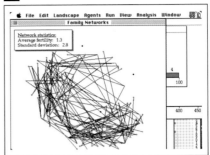

9

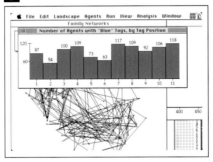

10

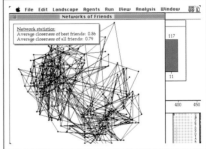

11

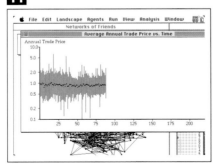

12

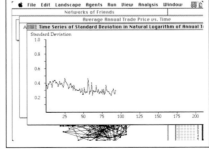

Animation VI-1. *Continued*

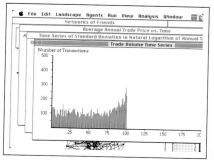

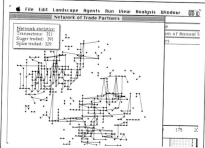

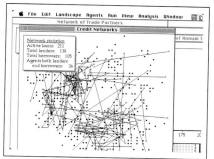

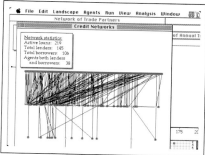

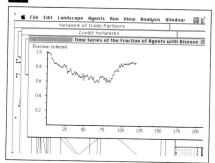

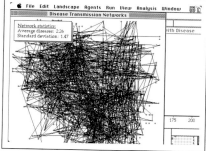

These are different perspectives on the *same* artificial society, with everything going at once.

As noted in Chapter I, many have bemoaned the artificial decomposition of social science into separate disciplines—economics, demography, cultural anthropology, politics, even epidemiology. Yet, there has been no "natural methodology" for studying these phenomena in a unified way. Some social scientists have taken highly aggregated—top-down—mathematical models of national economies, political systems, and so on and have "linked" them, yielding megamodels that have been criticized on a variety of grounds.[2] Unfortunately, attacks on particular models can have the effect of discrediting *interdisciplinary inquiry itself.*

Interdisciplinary research remains crucially important, and bottom-up modeling offers an alternative approach. As we have demonstrated, in an agent-based model each individual can have a variety of behavioral rules, and these can all be active simultaneously. When such multifaceted agents are released into an environment in which (and *with* which) they interact, the resulting society will—unavoidably—couple demography, economics, cultural change, conflict, and public health. All these spheres of *social* life will emerge—and merge—naturally and without top-down specification, from the purely local interactions of the individual agents. Because the individual is multifaceted, so is the society. The fixed coefficients of aggregate models—such as fertility rates or savings rates—become dynamic, emergent entities in bottom-up models. Indeed, had agent-based modeling been possible in the days of Thomas Robert Malthus, one wonders whether the fields of economics and demography would have developed so separately. In any event, the new techniques offer arresting demonstrations of how misleading the standard social science boundaries can be. Before giving a more focussed example of this, let us conduct a *gedanken* experiment.

Imagine that, instead of beginning the run with all behavioral rules turned on, as in the example above, we had continuously displayed a single variable—total population, for instance—while *sequentially* turning on each behavioral rule. At the outset, only the movement rule would be operative, and we would see the population plot descend from its initial level to the carrying capacity level. But then, if we turn on sexual reproduction the population will grow. If we then turn on diseases it

---

2. For example, see Simon [1990] and Nordhaus [1992].

will initially fall.[3] If we then turn credit on it will rise.[4] Quite clearly, we will see major perturbations in the population trajectory as we turn on each new behavioral rule. Indeed, this should be rather humbling to those who would attempt to study "demography" in isolation from other spheres of social activity.

In particular, is it sensible to study long-range population dynamics as though economic structure were irrelevant? Although you can probably guess our answer, we offer the following, especially arresting, demonstration of the point.

Indecomposability

The demonstration compares two evolutions of the same society: In one the agents do not trade while in the other they do. Society consists of an initial population of 500 agents inhabiting Chapter IV's sugar and spice landscape. The agents follow movement rule **M** and reproduce according to **S**. In the first run there is no trading. This population crashes, as shown in animation VI-2.

Next, with everything exactly as it was in animation VI-2, we make one simple change: We turn trade rule **T** on. How will this affect the history of society? Will it still crash? Will it fall monotonically to some positive steady state? Will society grow to some carrying capacity? The answer is given in animation VI-3.

And the correct answer is: None of the above! Initially, the population declines as in the no-trade case. Indeed, a statistician confronted with a time series for the first seventy-five years would likely project a repeat of that case. But society pulls out of its demographic nose dive and begins to grow. Indeed, it rises to a level more than twice that of the initial population. And then something even more surprising happens—a pattern of sustained oscillations sets in. Notice that the minima of these waves are still, at 700 agents, well above the initial population level. However, it is the period of the oscillations that is more interesting. The distance between peaks is roughly 115 years. The maximum lifetime of an agent, by contrast, is eighty years on average. In effect, no individual experiences the social pattern, the full cycle. Here, then, is an emergent social pattern, involving an "intergenerational" collaboration of agents,

---

3. Some agents die under the increased metabolic demands of disease.
4. Credit augments agent fertility.

Animation VI-2. Population Extinction under Rules ({**G**₁}, {**M, S**})

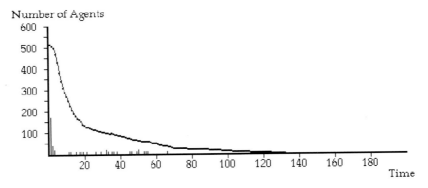

none of whom actually experiences the collective phenomenon.[5]

In light of these results, is it sensible to study long-range population dynamics in an economic vacuum, as though changes in economic structure had no effect on demographics? Quite clearly, the answer is no. Turning trade on made a dramatic difference in the population dynamics, so dramatic that it raises questions as to the very feasibility of a separate science of demography, that is, demography without some specification of economic regime.

As discussed in Chapter I, social science is hard because, among other things, certain kinds of experimentation are hard. As a case in point, in the real world we cannot command all agents to stop and start trading in order to gauge the effect on demographics of various trade regimes. But we can do this in agent-based models like Sugarscape. Obviously, the results depend on the model's particulars. But the mere fact that trade *can have* the effects displayed above suggests that economic policy *can be* a kind of population policy. At the very least, artificial societies raise important policy questions. And they may help answer some of them.

Complexity and Policy

In complex systems there may be highly indirect and counterintuitive ways to induce social outcomes from the bottom up. Combinations of small local reforms—"packages" exploiting precisely the nonlinear inter-

---

5. The same point applies to the population oscillations of Chapter III.

Animation VI-3. Near-Extinction Event Followed by Recovery to Long Waves under Rules ($\{G_1\}$, $\{M, S, T\}$)

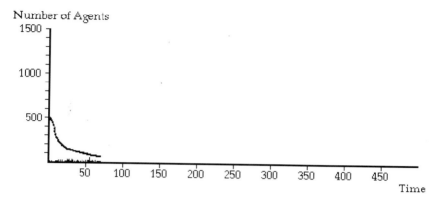

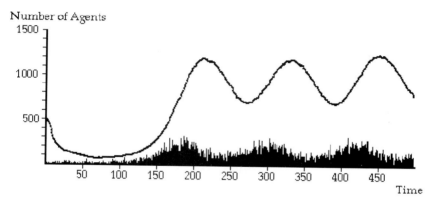

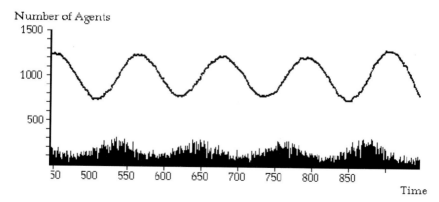

connectedness of things—may result in desirable outcomes in the large. Complexity beckons us to think this way.

Some Extensions of the Current Model

Overall, the agent-based approach—greatly facilitated by object-oriented programming and the explosive growth in computer performance—may yield *a new, more unified and evolutionary social science*, one in which migrations, demographic patterns, tribes and tribal conflict, epidemics, markets, firms, institutions, and governments all emerge from the bottom up. We see Sugarscape as a step in that direction. From here, there are many directions in which one might proceed. We have made preliminary steps in several of these directions and describe them presently.

Rule Ecologies and the "Fitness" of Maximization

Mathematical social science generally adopts two assumptions. First, agents can have different utility functions, but each agent's is *fixed*. Second, every one is assumed to be doing the *same* thing with its particular utility function—for example, maximizing it or maximizing its expected value. But across agents this behavioral rule is taken as invariant. In reality, of course, neither assumption makes much sense. In Chapter IV we relaxed the first of these assumptions, allowing individual utility functions to change due to cultural evolution (tag-flipping). But we did not explore the second assumption. In fact, artificial society models permit a more evolutionary outlook: Instead of assuming one behavioral rule, there could be a population of rules in society. One might specify this rule population at the outset [Arthur 1994] or have agents invent their own rules using genetic algorithms, genetic programming, or neural networks. But, however one generates the rules, some rules enjoy *differential survivability* over others—after a long time one observes more agents following rule i than following rule j. This really is all we can operationally mean when we assert that rule i enjoys a selective advantage over, or is "fitter than," rule j. A rule that enjoys a selective advantage over competitors in one environment may *not* enjoy that advantage in a different environment [Arthur *et al.*, 1994]; and crucially, the interaction of the agents—the ecology of rules—constantly changes the environment. We have every reason to believe, moreover, that this coupling between agents and their environment is a highly nonlinear one. It may be that some rule—"eat all you can today"—does extremely well for a long time, but then suddenly induces a radical transformation of its environment. And in that new environment that same rule may be highly maladapted.[6] The picture, then, is a coevolutionary one:

- Agent society represents an evolving rule ecology;
- The rule ecology constantly restructures its environment;
- The environment selects among rules and thereby restructures agent society;
- The process repeats.

There is a coevolution of agent society (the ecology of rules, phenotypes) and its environment. Now, it may well be that in some environments the rule "maximize individual utility (for example, sugar intake) in the current period" enjoys a selective advantage over other rules. But there seems to be little basis for asserting this as a general law.

A Definition of "Sustainability"

In this context, when people say that some behavior—a rule—is "unsustainable," they mean that continued operation under the relevant behavioral rule will transform the environment—perhaps quite suddenly and irreversibly—into one that is highly inhospitable to agents obeying that rule. If rule adjustment is slow in coming, then catastrophe, even extinction, can result. If all fishermen maximize profit in the current period, do they so deplete the fish stocks (transform their environment) that they ultimately suffer bankruptcy—economic extinction? Agents fishing in a different marine ecosystem who adopt some other rule may enjoy a long-term selective advantage. Admonitions that the human race is "driving without headlights" or "driving off cliffs" are analogies to this sort of outcome. The deep point is that *our rules create the cliffs we drive off.* Computational systems such as Sugarscape can offer "headlights," if you will, by permitting us to project, however crudely, the evolutionary consequences of certain rules. In any event, one exten-

---

6. A particularly powerful example of this occurs in the model of Ackley and Littman [1992] in which they populate their artificial world with a group of very capable but fiercely competitive agents and find that the population stays small and eventually goes extinct. When less capable agents are released into the same environment, their population rises and lasts indefinitely.

sion of the present work is to study the coevolution of rule ecologies and their environments.

Artificial Agents + Real Landscapes = Hybrid Models

In all of the foregoing discussion we have been talking about autonomous adaptive agents interacting in, and with, a completely artificial environment, that is, one that follows rules that we devise. It might be instructive to put the agents in a "real" environment—that is to say, a physically realistic environmental model. When the agents emit a pollutant it might be fed into an air-quality model, or groundwater toxification code, which would feed back into the agents' subsequent behavior, and so on. Such systems could be quite useful in alerting us to counterintuitive, nonlinear effects (good and bad) of various regulatory policies or technological changes.

Computational Archaeology

With artificial agents in a simple environmental model it might be possible to grow a history that mimics the true history of some ancient tribe as it migrated in response to environmental changes. At the time of this writing, we are collaborating with archeologists at the Santa Fe Institute and the Tree Ring Laboratory at the University of Arizona on a project whose aim is to grow the population dynamics and settlement patterns of the Anasazi from 400 to 1400 AD in the Long House Valley area of Black Mesa,[7] using environmental and demographic data reconstructed by archeological methods.[8]

Surely, viewing the development of artificial society modeling techniques from an evolutionary point of view, it makes more sense to start with relatively simple forms of production and organization than to attempt to "grow" New York City circa 2000 AD. And frankly, if, from a policy standpoint, we are worried about the combined effects of explosive population growth and rapid environmental change in the developing world, doing so is probably more useful in any case.

Ultimately, one would like to see if wage labor, firms, elaborate production hierarchies, and various forms of specialization (division of

---

7. In present-day northeastern Arizona.

8. Other agent-based models in archeology include the Mesa Verde Region Project [Gumerman and Kohler, 1996] and the EOS Project [Doran *et al.*, 1994].

labor) can be made to emerge in agent-based models. But, in the near term we would be happy with far more modest results.

Other Artificial Societies

In the proto-history of Chapter III we "grew" Red and Blue tribes through cultural tag-flipping. But, the artificial societies approach lets us study social pattern formation in many other ways. We provide two examples below.

A Variant of Schelling's Segregation Model

In Chapter I, Thomas Schelling's simple model of segregation [Schelling 1969, 1971a, 1971b, 1978] was mentioned as an early and prescient example of agent-based modeling in the social sciences.[9] He created both one- and two-dimensional landscapes populated with agents of two distinct "colors," and studied how micro-level agent preferences for like-colored neighbors manifested themselves at the macro-level. He posed various questions. What is the connection between individual prejudice and observed patterns of spatial segregation? Is it possible to get highly segregated settlement patterns even if *most* individuals are, in fact, color-blind?

We have implemented a variant of Schelling's model. Most aspects of our model are identical to his: every agent is a member of one or another group (here either Red or Blue) and has a fixed preference for like-colored neighbors. Here, a preference is simply a minimum percentage. For example, a Blue agent might insist that at least half of its neighbors also be Blue; in that case, its preference would be 50 percent. Each agent's behavior is governed by the following rule.

  Schelling's agent movement rule:
  - The agent computes the fraction of neighbors who are its own color;
  - If this number is greater than or equal to its preference the agent is considered satisfied, in which case end, else continue;
  - The agent looks for the nearest unoccupied lattice site that satisfies its preference and moves there.

---

9. For recent discussions of this model, see Binmore [1992: 393–95], Casti [1994: 213–15], and Krugman [1996: 15-21].

Some aspects of our implementation are slightly different from Schelling's: He uses the Moore neighborhood, whereas we use the von Neumann neighborhood; he moves agents to the *nearest* satisfactory site, whereas our agents simply select an acceptable site at random; his landscape has a finite boundary, whereas ours is a torus.[10]

As a first example of this model we randomly populate a 50 x 50 lattice (2500 sites) with 2000 Red and Blue agents in approximately equal numbers. This amounts to leaving 20 percent of the sites vacant. Each agent wishes at least 25 percent of its neighbors to be of its own color. Initially, many agents will be dissatisfied with their (randomly assigned) location. Each agent executes the rule above. The movement of an agent to a new location can make its new neighbors dissatisfied. Those who are newly dissatisfied are then permitted to move, and so on. This process repeats until all agents are satisfied, and so no further movement of agents occurs—that is, an equilibrium state is reached. A typical run is displayed in animation VI-4. Notice that the final configuration is significantly less random—more segregated—than the initial one.

Next, we sophisticate this simple model somewhat. The final quiescent state of animation VI-4 results from, in effect, infinite agent lifetimes: Once an equilibrium configuration is reached there is nothing to perturb this state. By making the maximum agent lifetime finite, so that agents depart the landscape once they have been there some length of time, the settlement pattern changes perpetually, never settling down.

In animation VI-5 all agents want at least 25 percent of their neighbors to be of their own color, as in animation VI-4, but now all agents are given a randomly assigned maximum lifetime between 80 and 100 time periods.[11] Once an agent reaches its maximum age it is removed and the population is kept constant by replacing it with a new agent of random color. This agent is placed at a randomly selected position satisfying its preference for neighbors.

Note that the long-run pattern of segregation is different from that shown in animation VI-4, but the degree of segregation is comparable.

Now we increase agent preferences for like neighbors and see how this affects the overall pattern of segregation. In particular, giving all agents the preference that at least 50 percent of their neighbors be of their own color, animation VI-6 results. Although every agent will tolerate config-

---

10. Neighborhood definitions were given in the neighbor networks section of Chapter II.

11. Here, "maximum lifetime" is interpreted as the point at which an agent decides to move to another landscape altogether; maximum residence duration is an equivalent notion.

Animation VI-4. Typical Evolution of the Schelling Model with
Agents Demanding at Least 25 Percent of Like Neighbors

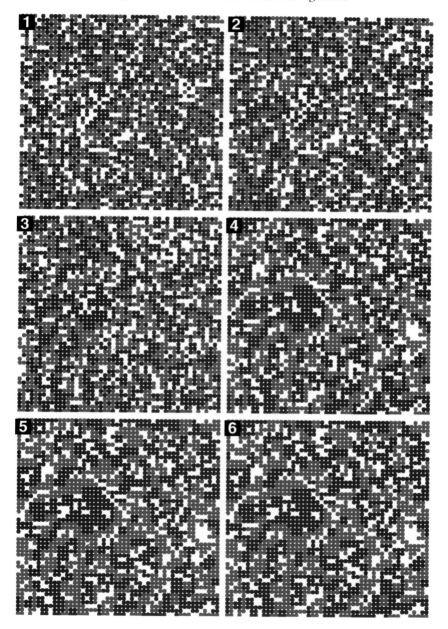

Animation VI-5. Typical Evolution of the Schelling Model with Agents Demanding at Least 25 Percent of Like Neighbors and Maximum Lifetimes Uniformly Distributed between 80 and 100

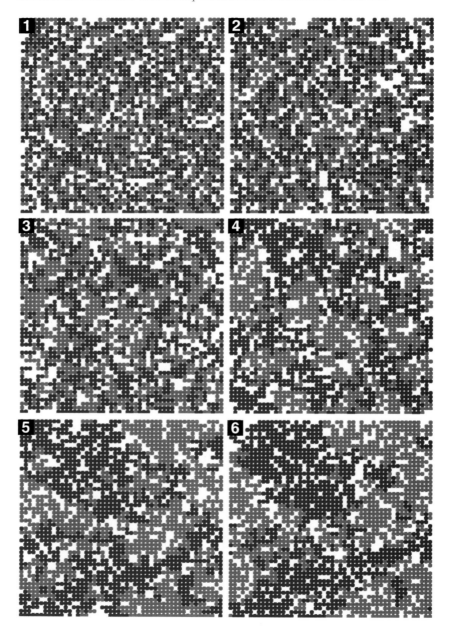

Animation VI-6. Typical Evolution of the Schelling Model with
Agents Demanding at Least 50 Percent of Like Neighbors and
Maximum Lifetimes Uniformly Distributed between 80 and 100

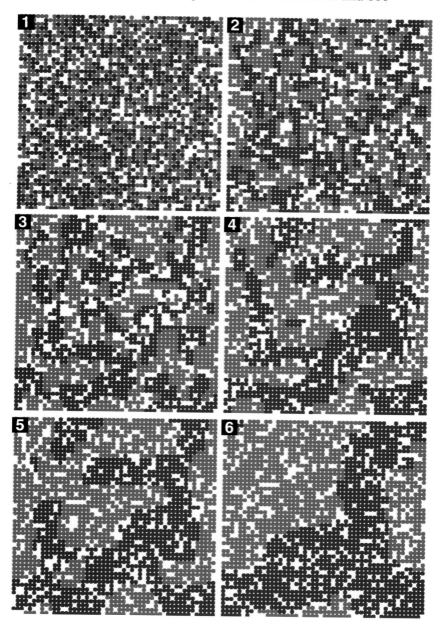

urations in which fully half of their neighbors are *not* of their own color, a high degree of segregation results, far higher than in the previous runs.

Outcomes of this type—in which a relatively small change in individual preferences leads to a large change in macro segregation patterns—were discovered by Schelling using little more than a checkerboard and rolls of pennies and dimes. Schelling also studied the effects of absolute population size, differing Red-Blue relative population sizes, and unequal inter-group preferences. One thing he did not study, however, is the effect of *intra-group* preference heterogeneity; this is hard to keep track of when iterating the model by hand. But it is easy to implement heterogeneous preferences and study their effects in a computer model where each agent is a distinct *object*. As a final example, then, we distribute agent preferences for like neighbors uniformly between 25 percent and 50 percent. This adds more tolerant individuals to the previous run. Will the final picture more closely resemble the modestly segregated outcome of animation VI-5, or the more completely segregated society of animation VI-6? Animation VI-7 provides the answer.

Adding this degree of tolerance is *not sufficient to generate* desegregation—indeed, a highly segregated pattern endures.

Now, had you been *shown* this terminal pattern—the already emerged phenomenon—of segregation, you might well have concluded that virtually every agent had demanded that all neighbors be of its color. Not so! The question, then, is this: How *little* racism is enough to "tip" a society into this segregated pattern? In turn, is racial segregation reversible through "invasion" by a handful of "color-blind" individuals? How much does it take to "tip" things the other way? Do these simple models help explain why we are so often surprised by the *true* preference landscapes—for example, the Serb-Bosnian one—that burst forth when suppressive institutions are suddenly dismantled?

If we want to understand political change, we need ways to study the "match" between political institutions and the underlying preference landscapes. When the match is good, there is political stability, but when the match is bad, frustration accumulates and there can be sudden releases of conflictual energy.

Ring World

Ring World is yet another artificial society. Here, the landscape is a *circle* of sugar sites. The agents are once again sugar harvesters, but their rules of behavior are simpler than in Sugarscape. First, agents search *only* in

Animation VI-7. Typical Evolution of the Schelling Model with Agent Demands for Like Neighbors Uniformly Distributed between 25 Percent and 50 Percent, and Maximum Lifetimes Uniformly Distributed between 80 and 100

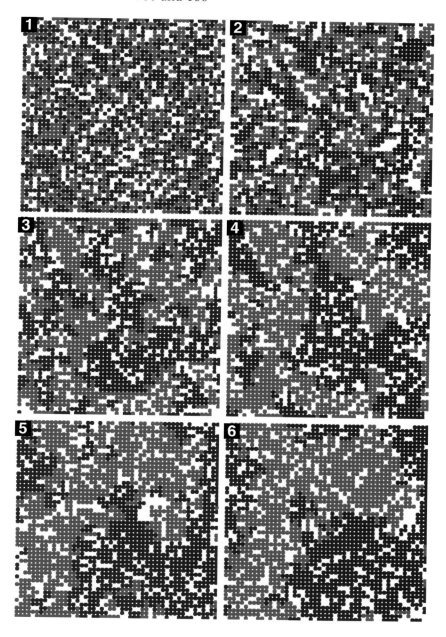

the counterclockwise direction on the sugar ring. Each agent has vision randomly chosen from some range (15 to 30 in the animations here). Subject to these strictures, the agent rule is: *Inspect all unoccupied sites within your vision, select the nearest site with maximum sugar, go there and eat the sugar.* As for the ring, there are 150 sites. Initially, the sugar level is distributed randomly between values of 0 and 4, and 40 agents are distributed randomly around the ring. The rule for the sites is that sugar grows back at unit rate to a capacity value, which is 4 in the animations below. There is no death, birth, combat, cultural transmission, disease, or trade; no attention is paid to sugar accumulation. Each agent moves once each time period; agents are called in random order. What could possibly happen? The answer is given in animation VI-8.

Remarkably, the agents cluster into groups. Often they separate into groups of comparable size! Notice, moreover, that agents who are hopping along quite slowly are ultimately absorbed, swept up, into faster-moving groups. They move faster when they are part of a group. Now, let us play a familiar game. Imagine that the rules these agents are executing had not been stated in advance and that you had been shown this emergent "flocking" behavior and were asked, "What are the agents' rules?" Most people would offer rules explicitly including something about other agents or groups; for example, "join the smallest cluster that is surrounded by sugar," or perhaps some other rule of this sort. However, the seemingly "social" behavior (the clustering) is not driven by any social impulse but is solely a *product of the agent-environment coupling.*

Here we started with agents randomly distributed and they agglomerated into cliques. What if we start with all agents in one megagroup (of 40)? Will they disaggregate into like-sized cliques?[12] The answer is "yes," as shown in animation VI-9.

A notable property of social organizations—from ant colonies to the Supreme Court—is that their memberships change while important elements of their structure do not. The groups that form on the ring have this "organizational" property, albeit in a simple form; their agent composition is fluid while their outstanding structural feature—their size—is approximately constant.

---

12. We thank Bruce Blair for this question.

Animation VI-8. Flocking on the Ring

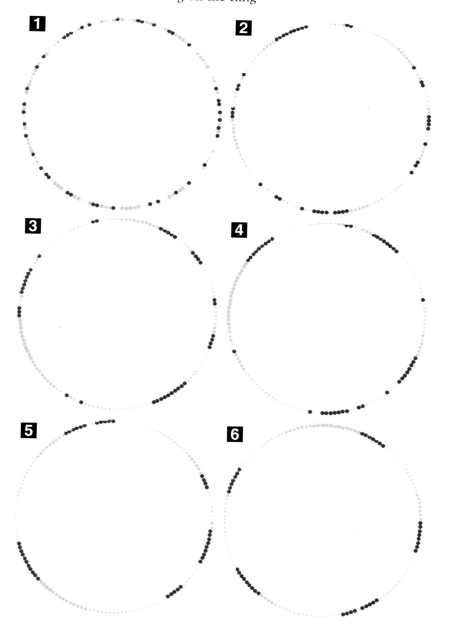

Animation VI-9. Disaggregation to Groups

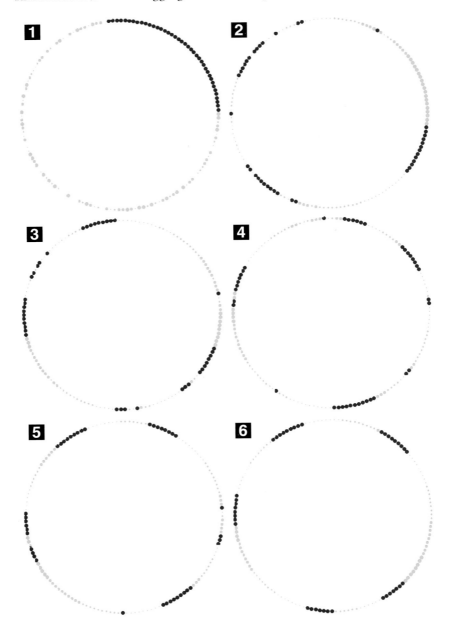

Analysis

To understand the basic clustering phenomenon, imagine the same sugar ring, but with a population of exactly two agents, each having vision of 10, say. Suppose these two agents start out as neighbors, a clique of two. And to make the idea as clear as possible, imagine that all sugar sites grow back to a value of 4 once all agents have moved. Will this clique stay together? Start with the "follower." It looks out 10 sites counterclockwise, disqualifying the immediately adjacent site since it is occupied, and notes that (since they all have sugar value of 4) the *nearest* unoccupied site with maximum sugar is the one just in front of the "leader." So, it "leapfrogs" to that site and eats the sugar. Of course, the former leader now becomes the follower and, by the same argument, does the same thing. So the two of them "tread" around the ring, perpetually leapfrogging one another along the way. When the "leader" moves first it moves just one site forward. But when the "follower" moves it will jump to the site immediately ahead of the "leader" since that is the first site having maximum sugar. So we see from first principles that the agents do stay together once they (randomly) encounter one another.[13] Now consider a threesome. It is easy to see that the same thing occurs with three agents as with two. This holds all the way up to N agents, where the maximum value of N is related to the vision of the most nearsighted agent in the group. The size of a group is constrained by the requirement that the most nearsighted be able to see to the front of the group when it is that (most myopic) agent's turn to move. This, in turn, is the reason the megacluster of forty agents (*none* of whose vision is forty) breaks up!

This is also how agents that are loping along by themselves get swept up into faster-moving clusters. An agent with vision of, say, 10 is hopping along by itself when along swoops a flock of five agents, which glides right over it. Now, suppose this lone agent's turn comes up precisely as the flock passes by, so that the nearest best *unoccupied* site it can see is exactly at the head of the flock. The agent then leapfrogs to the

---

13. This simple exposition is written as though agents take turns moving. Actually, in Ring World, the call order is randomized each time through the agent list. Under random call order, gaps can open between agents. Hence, the more precise statement is that *if* agents are observed to tread around together *then* it is a result of the leapfrogging mechanism described in the text. While couplings between particular agents can break down under random call order, clique formation itself is not artifactual; it is robust to randomization of the call order.

head of the pack, and thereafter stays in it—now going much faster than it had been going alone. This is exactly how groups form in Ring World.

The number, size, and permanence of groups is, however, sensitive to the distribution of sugar capacities on the ring and the distribution of vision in agent society. In some cases, essentially no groups form. By contrast, under certain configurations, a few wildly fast groups race around, intermittently "shedding" agents, while cascades of slower metastable cliques take shape and dissipate. All this from such a simple model! This serves as yet more evidence of the fertility of the artificial societies approach.

Formal Analysis of Artificial Societies

At various points we have offered detailed quantitative analyses of data generated in the Sugarscape model—data on prices and wealth distributions, for example. The ability to generate noiseless data is a powerful feature of artificial societies. In addition to this kind of empirical study, it is desirable to pursue formal analyses—outright theorems and proofs—where possible. While the exact evolution of *individual* agents and sites seems analytically intractable, certain probabilistic analyses are possible.

For example, when our model is specialized to an environment of randomly distributed resources and fixed agent density, the distribution of the number of neighbors that the agents have can be determined analytically from first principles. Then, for sites having capacities varying in accord with a known distribution function, it is possible to calculate the equilibrium distribution of resource levels when the number and types of agents are known. From this information, the equilibrium distribution of agent income can be determined. When the income distribution is combined with initial endowment and age distributions, a distribution of wealth can be deduced. It is also possible to describe various aspects of cultural tag-flipping relating to the overall distribution of tags. When a second resource is added to the landscape and agents move according to a wealth-dependent welfare function, the distribution of wealth implies a distribution of marginal rates of substitution of one resource for the other. Finally, when agents are permitted to trade one resource for the other, an expression for the distribution of annual trade volume and annual price can be derived from the previously calculated distributions for the number of neighbors, wealth, and *MRS*.

However, this is a highly special case. When the environment is structured (not random), when sex is "on" (and agent density is fluctuating), when diseases, combat, culture, and credit are active, then analytical results are much harder to come by. It is our hope that, ultimately, interesting artificial societies will inspire the development of entirely new formal methods of analysis.

Generative Social Science

It may be useful to enter into a brief philosophical discussion. From an epistemological standpoint, what "sort of science" are we doing when we build artificial societies like Sugarscape? Clearly, agent-based social science does not seem to be either deductive or inductive in the usual senses. But then what is it? We think *generative* is an appropriate term. The aim is to provide initial microspecifications (initial agents, environments, and rules) that are *sufficient to generate* the macrostructures of interest.[14] We consider a given macrostructure to be "explained" by a given microspecification when the latter's generative sufficiency has been established.[15] As suggested in Chapter I, we interpret the question, "can you explain it?" as asking "can you grow it?" In effect, *we are proposing a generative program for the social sciences and see the artificial society as its principal scientific instrument.*

We hope the potential power of the artificial societies approach has been demonstrated. At the same time, it is important to consider the potential limits—both practical and theoretical—intrinsic to this approach. At the time of this writing the practical upper limit on the number of agents which extant computer hardware is capable of simulating is on the order of 10^5–10^7 when the agents have relatively simple behavior and as low as 10^2–10^4 when agent behavior is even modestly complex. While this situation is sure to improve, it may be a long time before simulation with large numbers of complex agents is feasible.

---

14. Of course, we may also be interested in generating future *agents*, so initial microspecifications may be required to generate later microstates. Generative is the point, not macro, *per se*. We use the term in much the same way Chomsky does. As Casti explains, "the grammar of each language must be *generative* in the sense that it must be a set of rules capable of "generating" all the well-formed (i.e., grammatical) sentences of the language and none of the ill-formed ones." Casti [1989: 215].

15. As just noted, some such demonstrations take the form of outright proofs. Others take the form of simulations. There are various levels at which generative sufficiency can be established; see Axtell and Epstein [1994].

A deeper issue for social science is that there may be *theoretical* limits to what is knowable in such computational sytems as artificial societies. These limits will have to do with *computability, decidability, NP completeness*, and other properties of algorithms, active areas of research in logic, computer science, and automata theory generally. For example, it is known that the computational task of a Walrasian auctioneer—computing a Brouwer fixed-point—has worst case complexity that is exponential in the number of commodities.[16] In some areas, it may be that simulation *really is* the best we can do.[17]

Looking Ahead . . .

Just as the community of biologists had to *learn* to fully exploit the microscope when it was first invented, so we have only begun to explore the uses and limits of the artificial society as a scientific tool. We can only hope that the field itself will display the evolutionary process it studies— new agents join, and intellectual heterogeneity grows; social networks of scientists endogenously take shape;[18] selection pressures operate; and from the social enterprise of agent-based social science, interesting things emerge!

---

16. Scarf [1973] conjectured that typical running times for the computation of Walrasian equilibria is $O(n^4)$, where n is the dimension of the commodity space. That the worst case performance is exponential in n is proved in Hirsch, Papadimitriou, and Varasis [1989]. Subsequently, Papadimitriou [1994] has pointed out that existence of Brouwer and Kakutani fixed points—and thus Walrasian equilibria—is established by constructive arguments based on exponentially large graphs, and has characterized these problems with new complexity classes.

17. For example, Buss, Papadimitriou, and Tsitsiklis [1991] have studied systems of identical automata coupled through a global control rule. They find that when rules are anonymous (do not depend on the state of any particular automaton) then the system is predictible. However, when the global rule is nonanonymous then the future state of the system is PSPACE complete, and there is a very real sense in which simulation constitutes the best analysis possible for such systems.

18. Various developments can facilitate this. Standards can simplify code sharing and inter-model comparison. When objects from one model can be imported into other models, "docking experiments" of the sort reported in Axtell *et al.* [1996] are facilitated. General purpose agent-based development environments, such as the Santa Fe Institute's SWARM, may also expand the community of agent-based modelers.

Appendix A
Software Engineering Aspects of Artificial Societies

Here we briefly describe some software engineering aspects of the artificial society known as Sugarscape. This artificial world is composed of two main elements: a population of agents and the environment on which the agents "live." Of the many ways in which these might be implemented in software, we have found object-oriented programming (OOP) to be a particularly natural development environment for Sugarscape specifically and artificial societies generally. Each object in OOP has both internal states, called instance variables, and behavioral rules, so-called methods.[1] Agents as well as individual environmental sites are objects in Sugarscape.

The sugarscape proper is implemented as a two-dimensional array of sites. Each site object has among its instance variables its current resource levels and capacities (both n-dimensional vectors, where n is user-specified), its pollution levels and fluxes (both m-vectors, m specified by the user), and a reference to its occupant (a pointer to an agent object[2]). It also has methods for resource growth, pollution deposition and transport (for example, diffusion), and visual display. Each site's methods use information contained in its instance variables, and possibly state information from neighboring sites. For example, Chapter II's pollution diffusion rule requires that each site get information from its von Neumann neighbors in determining next period's flux. This coupling of sites through methods makes the sugarscape a cellular automaton.

The environment as a whole, the sugarscape lattice, is also implemented as an object. It has instance variables concerning the overall

---

1. For an introduction to OOP, see Booch [1994].
2. The Sugarscape code was developed on the Macintosh, and due to the way the Mac operating system deals with memory, so-called "handles" (pointers to pointers) are actually used instead of pointers whenever one object must refer to another object.

state of the sites (average resource and pollution levels, for example), and methods for computing these statistics.

Agents are also objects. Instance variables for agents include vision, metabolism (an n-vector), location (pointer to a site object), resource accumulations (an n-vector), current age, ages related to childbearing (puberty age, for example), death age, identity of parents (pointers), cultural tags (a binary string), and an immune system (a binary string). Agent objects are maintained in a linked list and so each agent also has pointers to neighboring agents in the list.[3] Furthermore, when agents are ranked, as from poorest to richest in the computation of a Gini coefficient, these rankings are kept in a linked list and so each agent has pointers to neighboring agents in the ranked list. Each agent has further instance variables that are pointers to list objects, such as its list of children, a list of friends, lists related to borrowing and lending, and a list of diseases with which it is afflicted. Agent methods include all behavioral rules (movement, pollution production, sexual reproduction, inheritance, cultural transmission, group membership, combat, trade, credit, immune response, disease transmission) as well as related procedures (for example, the welfare and *MRS* functions). Other methods include specialized routines for agent display. In total, each agent has over 100 methods.

The reader familiar with OOP might wonder how this large agent object is actually declared. There is a definite sense in which Chapter II's simple agent, who does little more than move and pollute, can be used as a superclass for definition of Chapter III's sexually reproducing agent. That is, we might define a "ChapterIIIAgent" as a descendent of the simple "ChapterIIAgent," with the former inheriting all of the latter's instance variables and methods. Then Chapter IV's trading agent would be a descendent of the "ChapterIIIAgent" and so on. This design was explored but efficiency considerations led us to the less elaborate design of a single agent class specification.

There is also an object for the population of agents as a whole. It has instance variables relating to aggregate population statistics (average age and fertility, minimum agent wealth, and maximum inheritance gift, for example) and methods for computing these. It also keeps track of the first agent in the overall agent list as well as the highest and lowest

---

3. The reader unfamiliar with linked lists should consult any book on data structures; see Sedgewick [1983: 25–28]

ranked agents in the ranked list. The agent population object also encapsulates methods for sorting and searching the agents according to any one of various criteria. Given that the population is constantly changing due to agent birth and death, it was found that a primitive kind of census was needed to keep track of the agent population, and both census information and survey routines are part of this larger population object.

Many other object definitions exist in the Sugarscape software, including objects for special agents (representative and observational agents, for example), agent and site groups (such as all Blue agents and all sites in the southwest), graphs (social networks), and plotting (histograms, time series, supply-demand plot). The modularity afforded by these and many other objects was crucial to managing the complexity of the 20,000 lines of code that make up Sugarscape.

Appendix B
Summary of Rule Notation

<u>Symbol</u>	<u>Name</u>	<u>Definition</u>
G_α	Sugarscape growback	• At each lattice position, sugar grows back at a rate of α units per time interval up to the capacity at that position.
M	Agent movement	• Look out as far as vision permits in each of the four lattice directions, north, south, east, and west; • Considering only unoccupied lattice positions, find the nearest position producing maximum welfare; • Move to the new position; • Collect all the resources at that location.
$\mathbf{R}_{[a,b]}$	Agent replacement	When an agent dies it is replaced by an agent of age 0 having random genetic attributes, random position on the sugarscape, random initial endowment, and a maximum age selected from the range [a,b].
$\mathbf{S}_{\alpha\beta\gamma}$	Seasonal growback	Initially it is *summer* in the top half of the sugarscape and *winter* in the bottom half. Then, every γ time periods the seasons flip—in the region where it was summer it becomes winter and vice versa. For each site, if the season is summer then sugar grows back at a rate of α units per time interval; if the season is winter then the growback rate is α units per β time intervals.
$\mathbf{P}_{\Pi,\mathbf{x}}$	Pollution formation	For n resources and m pollutants, when n-dimensional resource vector $\mathbf{r}$ is gathered from the sugarscape then m-dimensional production pollution vector $\mathbf{p}$ is produced according to $\mathbf{p} = \Pi\mathbf{r}$, where Π is an m x n matrix; when n-dimensional (metabolism) vector $\mathbf{m}$ is consumed then m-dimensional consumption pollution vector $\mathbf{c}$ is produced

according to $c = \mathbf{Xm}$, where $\mathbf{X}$ is an m x n matrix. (This generalizes the rule given in Chapter II.)

$\mathbf{D}_\alpha$	Pollution diffusion	• Each α time periods and at each site, compute the pollution flux—the average pollution level over all von Neumann neighboring sites; • Each site's flux becomes its new pollution level.
$\mathbf{S}$	Agent mating	• Select a neighboring agent at random; • If the neighboring agent is of the opposite sex *and* if both agents are fertile *and* at least one of the agents has an empty neighboring site *then* a newborn is produced by crossing-over the parents' genetic and cultural characteristics; • Repeat for all neighbors.
$\mathbf{I}$	Agent inheritance	When an agent dies its wealth is equally divided among all its living children.
none	Agent cultural transmission	• Select a neighboring agent at random; • Select a tag randomly; • If the neighbor agrees with the agent at that tag position, no change is made; if they disagree, the neighbor's tag is flipped to agree with the agent's tag; • Repeat for all neighbors.
none	Group membership	Agents are defined to be members of the Blue group when 0s outnumber 1s on their tag strings, and members of the Red group in the opposite case.
$\mathbf{K}$	Agent culture	Combination of "agent cultural transmission" and "agent group membership" rules given immediately above.
$\mathbf{C}_\alpha$	Agent combat	• Look out as far as vision permits in the four principal lattice directions; • Throw out all sites occupied by members of the agent's own tribe; • Throw out all sites occupied by members of different tribes who are wealthier than the agent; • The reward of each remaining site is given by the resource level at the site plus, if it is occupied, the minimum of α and the occupant's wealth; • Throw out all sites that are vulnerable to retaliation;

- Select the nearest position having maximum reward and go there;
- Gather the resources at the site plus the minimum of α and the occupant's wealth, if the site was occupied;
- If the site was occupied, then the former occupant is considered "killed"—permanently removed from play.

T   Agent trade

- Agent and neighbor compute their *MRS*s; if these are equal then end, else continue;
- The direction of exchange is as follows: spice flows from the agent with the higher *MRS* to the agent with the lower *MRS* while sugar goes in the opposite direction;
- The geometric mean of the two *MRS*s is calculated—this will serve as the bargaining price, *p*;
- The quantities to be exchanged are as follows: if $p > 1$ then p units of spice for 1 unit of sugar; if $p < 1$ then $1/p$ units of sugar for 1 unit of spice;
- If this trade will (a) make both agents better off (increases the welfare of both agents), and (b) not cause the agents' *MRS*s to cross over one another, then the trade is made and return to start, else end.

L$_{dr}$ Agent credit

- An agent is a *potential lender* if it is too old to have children, in which case *the maximum amount it may lend is one-half of its current wealth*;
- An agent is a *potential lender* if it is *of* childbearing age and has wealth in excess of the amount necessary to have children, in which case *the maximum amount it may lend is the excess wealth*;
- An agent is a *potential borrower* if it is of childbearing age *and* has insufficient wealth to have a child *and* has income (resources gathered, minus metabolism, minus other loan obligations) in the present period making it credit-worthy for a loan written at terms specified by the lender;
- If a potential borrower and a potential lender are neighbors then a loan is origi-

nated with a duration of d years at the rate of r percent, and the face value of the loan amount is transferred from the lender to the borrower;

• At the time of the loan due date, if the borrower has sufficient wealth to repay the loan then a transfer from the borrower to the lender is made; else the borrower is required to pay back half of its wealth and a new loan is originated for the remaining sum;

• If the borrower on an active loan dies before the due date then the lender simply takes a loss;

• If the lender on an active loan dies before the due date then the borrower is not required to pay back the loan, unless inheritance rule **I** is active, in which case the lender's children now become the borrower's creditors.

none	Agent immune response	• If the disease is a substring of the immune system then end (the agent is immune), else (the agent is infected) go to the following step; • The substring in the agent immune system having the smallest Hamming distance from the disease is selected and the first bit at which it is different from the disease string is changed to match the disease.
none	Disease transmission	For each neighbor, a disease that currently afflicts the agent is selected at random and given to the neighbor.
E	Agent disease processes	Combination of "agent immune response" and "agent disease transmission" rules given immediately above.

Appendix C
State-Dependence of the Welfare Function

The utility function described in Chapter IV is not a traditional one insofar as its arguments are the *wealths* of the two commodities, sugar and spice. One way to interpret this function is as a state-dependent utility or welfare function. That is, as the agent accumulates wealth its preferences, as represented by the utility function, change in a systematic, well-defined way. In particular, a landscape of sugar and spice will look different in welfare terms to biologically identical agents when the only difference between them is their wealth. Similarly, an agent facing identical landscapes at different times in its life—say it was relatively poor early in its life and relatively prosperous later on—will value them differently. The way in which the utility function gives rise to this behavior is formally described in this appendix.

Consider an agent with equal metabolisms $(m_1 = m_2)$ and arbitrary wealths (w_1, w_2) and suppose that in its neighborhood the site preferred above all others has sugar and spice levels (x_1, x_2). Now assume that at a later date, when it has wealth (W_1, W_2), this agent is faced with the same (distribution of) sites. Under what conditions will it prefer a different site?

Theorem: Sites having sugar and spice levels $(x_1 - \Delta_1, x_2 + \Delta_2)$, where $\Delta_1 \Delta_2 > 0$, will be preferred to sites having levels (x_1, x_2) if

$$W_1 - w_1 > (<) \frac{\Delta_1}{\Delta_2} (W_2 - w_2)$$

for Δ_1 and Δ_2 positive (negative).

<u>Proof</u>: When the agent has wealth (w_1, w_2) the condition that (x_1, x_2) sites are preferred to $(x_1 - \Delta_1, x_2 + \Delta_2)$ sites is

186

$$(w_1 + x_1)^{m_1}(w_2 + x_2)^{m_2} > (w_1 + x_1 - \Delta_1)^{m_1}(w_2 + x_2 + \Delta_2)^{m_2}.$$

Since we have stipulated that $m_1 = m_2$ this is equivalent to

$$(w_1 + x_1)(w_2 + x_2) > (w_1 + x_1 - \Delta_1)(w_2 + x_2 + \Delta_2).$$

Solving for Δ_1 this becomes

$$\Delta_1 > \frac{(w_1 + x_1)\Delta_2}{w_2 + x_2 + \Delta_2}.$$

For $\Delta_2 > 0$ this implies

$$\frac{\Delta_1}{\Delta_2} > \frac{w_1 + x_1}{w_2 + x_2 + \Delta_2}, \tag{C.1a}$$

while for $\Delta_2 < 0$

$$\frac{\Delta_1}{\Delta_2} < \frac{w_1 + x_1}{w_2 + x_2 + \Delta_2}. \tag{C.1b}$$

Later, when the agent has wealth (W_1, W_2), the $(x_1 - \Delta_1, x_2 + \Delta_2)$ site is preferred to the (x_1, x_2) site—the opposite of the previous case—and so it must be true that

$$\frac{\Delta_1}{\Delta_2} < \frac{W_1 + x_1}{W_2 + x_2 + \Delta_2} \tag{C.2a}$$

for $\Delta_2 > 0$ and

$$\frac{\Delta_1}{\Delta_2} > \frac{W_1 + x_1}{W_2 + x_2 + \Delta_2} \tag{C.2b}$$

for $\Delta_2 < 0$.

Now, for the case of $\Delta_2 > 0$, consider C.1a and C.2a to be inequalities with (x_1, x_2) the unknown quantities; the goal here is to solve for these. Alternatively, it must be true that the relationship between the six parameters of the problem—the four wealths and the two perturbations—cannot depend on (x_1, x_2). To accomplish this solve C.1a and C.2a for x_1 and there results

$$x_1 < \frac{\Delta_1}{\Delta_2}\left(w_2 + x_2 + \Delta_2\right) - w_1$$

$$x_1 > \frac{\Delta_1}{\Delta_2}\left(W_2 + x_2 + \Delta_2\right) - W_1.$$

Consider x_1 to be some number, as it will be at any particular site. Then these expressions imply that

$$\frac{\Delta_1}{\Delta_2}\left(w_2 + x_2 + \Delta_2\right) - w_1 > \frac{\Delta_1}{\Delta_2}\left(W_2 + x_2 + \Delta_2\right) - W_1.$$

Since x_2 and Δ_2 appear on both sides of this inequality it can be simplified to read

$$W_1 - w_1 > \frac{\Delta_1}{\Delta_2}\left(W_2 - w_2\right). \tag{C.3a}$$

Similarly, when $\Delta_2 < 0$ there results

$$W_1 - w_1 < \frac{\Delta_1}{\Delta_2}\left(W_2 - w_2\right). \tag{C.3b}$$

QED

A numerical example that illustrates site switching due to altered wealth states is given presently.

Example:

Consider an agent for whom $m_1 = m_2$ and who has wealth (20, 50) at time t_1. Among all sites in its vision the one which it prefers has (sugar, spice) levels (3, 3). At a later time, t_2, with wealth (150, 250) and facing the same distribution of sites that it may potentially inhabit, what types of sites will be preferred to (3, 3)?

Solution: Consider for the moment only sites produced by Δ_1 and $\Delta_2 > 0$, that is, sites on which there is relatively *less* sugar and *more* spice than (3, 3). Since $W_2 > w_2$ here, divide both sides of C.3a by $(W_2 - w_2)$, yielding

$$\frac{W_1 - w_1}{W_2 - w_2} > \frac{\Delta_1}{\Delta_2}.$$

Now substitute the agent wealths for (w_1, w_2) and (W_1, W_2) in the left hand side of this expression, giving

$$\frac{W_1 - w_1}{W_2 - w_2} = \frac{150 - 20}{250 - 50} = \frac{130}{200} = \frac{13}{20} > \frac{\Delta_1}{\Delta_2}.$$

One feasible pair of Δs is $(1, 2)$. Therefore, sites like $(x_1-1, x_2+2) = (2, 5)$ are preferred at the later time.

To check this just plug the numbers into the expression for agent welfare

$$W(20 + 3, 50 + 3) > W(20 + 2, 50 + 5).$$

Carrying through the calculations

$$23^{m_1}53^{m_2} > 22^{m_1}55^{m_2}$$

which implies $23 \cdot 53 > 22 \cdot 55$ in the case of equal exponents. This is indeed true since $1219 > 1210$. At the later time the alternative site is preferred. To see this, one carries out the following calculation

$$W(150 + 3, 250 + 3) < W(150 + 2, 250 + 5),$$

producing

$$153^{m_1}253^{m_2} < 152^{m_1}255^{m_2},$$

which is easily verified as true since $153 \cdot 253 = 38709 < 152 \cdot 255 = 38760$. Thus the site $(3, 3)$ is preferred by the agent at time t_1 and site $(2,5)$ is considered the better site at time t_2. The case of Δ_1 and $\Delta_2 < 0$ is similar.

References

Aaron, H. 1994. "Public Policy, Values, and Consciousness." *Journal of Economic Perspectives* 8 (2): 3–21.

Ackley, D. H., and M. L. Littman. 1992. "Learning from Natural Selection in an Artificial Environment." In *Artificial Life II Video Proceedings,* edited by C. G. Langton. Redwood City, Calif.: Addison-Wesley.

Albin, P., and D. K. Foley. 1990. "Decentralized, Dispersed Exchange without an Auctioneer: A Simulation Study." *Journal of Economic Behavior and Organization* 18 (1): 27–51.

An, M., and N. M. Kiefer. 1992. "Evolution and Equilibria Selection of Repeated Lattice Games." Working Paper. Cornell University, Department of Economics.

Anderlini, L., and A. Ianni. 1993a. "Path Dependence and Learning from Neighbours." Working Paper. Cambridge University, Faculty of Economics and Politics.

———. 1993b. "Local Learning on a Torus." Working Paper. Cambridge University, Faculty of Economics and Politics.

Anderson, P. W., K. J. Arrow, and D. Pines, eds. 1988. *The Economy as an Evolving Complex System.* Redwood City, Calif.: Addison-Wesley.

Anderson, R. M., and R. M. May. 1991. *Infectious Diseases of Humans: Dynamics and Control.* New York: Oxford University Press.

Arifovic, J. 1994. "Genetic Algorithm Learning and the Cobweb Model." *Journal of Economic Dynamics and Control* 18: 3–28.

Arifovic, J., and C. Eaton. 1995. "Coordination via Genetic Learning." *Computational Economics* 8: 181–203.

Arrow, K. 1994. "Methodological Individualism and Social Knowledge." *American Economic Review* 84 (2): 1–9.

Arrow, K., and F. Hahn. 1971. *General Competitive Analysis.* New York: North-Holland.

Arthur, W. B. 1988. "Self-Reinforcing Mechanisms in Economics." In *The Economy as an Evolving Complex System,* edited by P. W. Anderson, K. J. Arrow, and D. Pines. Redwood City, Calif.: Addison-Wesley.

———. 1990. "Positive Feedbacks in the Economy." *Scientific American* (February): 92–99.

———. 1991. "Designing Economic Agents That Act Like Human Agents: A Behavioral Approach to Bounded Rationality." *American Economic Review, Papers and Proceedings* 81 (2): 353–59.

————. 1994. "Inductive Reasoning and Bounded Rationality." *American Economic Review, Papers and Proceedings* 84 (2): 406–11.

Arthur, W. B., Yu. M. Ermoliev, and Yu. M. Kaniovski. 1987. "Path-Dependent Processes and the Emergence of Macrostructure." *European Journal of Operational Research* 30 (3): 294–303.

Arthur, W. B., *et al.* 1994. "An Artificial Stock Market." Working Paper. University of Wisconsin, Department of Economics.

Ashby, W. R. 1956. *An Introduction to Cybernetics.* Wiley.

Aubin, J-P. 1981. "A Dynamical, Pure Exchange Economy with Feedback Pricing." *Journal of Economic Behavior and Organization* 2: 95–127.

Axelrod, R. 1984. *The Evolution of Cooperation.* Basic Books.

————. 1987. "The Evolution of Strategies in the Iterated Prisoner's Dilemma." In *Genetic Algorithms and Simulated Annealing,* edited by L. Davis. Los Altos, Calif.: Morgan Kaufmann.

————. 1993. "A Model of the Emergence of New Political Actors." Working Paper 93-11-068. Sante Fe, N.M.: Santa Fe Institute.

————. 1995. "The Convergence and Stability of Cultures: Local Convergence and Global Polarization." Working Paper 95-03-028. Santa Fe, N.M.: Santa Fe Institute.

Axtell, R. L., and J. M. Epstein. 1994. "Agent-Based Modeling: Understanding Our Creations." *Bulletin of the Santa Fe Institute,* 9 (2): 28–32.

Axtell, R. L., *et al.* 1996. "Aligning Simulation Models: A Case Study and Results." *Computational and Mathematical Organization Theory* 1 (2): 123–41.

Baas, N. A. 1994. "Emergence, Hierarchies, and Hyperstructures." In *Artificial Life III,* edited by C. G. Langton. Redwood City, Calif.: Addison-Wesley.

Bak, P., K. Chen, and C. Tang. 1990. "A Forest-fire Model and Some Thoughts on Turbulence." *Physics Letters A* 147 (5-6): 297–300.

Bak, P., and C. Tang. 1989. "Earthquakes as a Self-Organized Critical Phenomenon." *Journal of Geophysical Research* 94 (B11): 15635–37.

Bala, V., and Majumdar, M. 1992. "Chaotic Tatonnement." *Economic Theory* 2: 437–45.

Bankes, S. 1994. "Exploring the Foundations of Artificial Societies: Experiments in Evolving Solutions to the Iterated N-player Prisoner's Dilemma." In *Artificial Life IV,* edited by R. Brooks and P. Maes. MIT Press.

Banks, D., and K. Carley. 1994a. "Metric Inference for Social Networks." *Journal of Classification* 11: 121–49.

————. 1994b. "Testing Alternative Models of Network Evolution." Working Paper. Carnegie Mellon University.

Benninga, S. 1992. "Non-Walrasian Equilibria with Speculation." *Journal of Economic Behavior and Organization* 17 (2): 241–56.

Bertsekas, D. P., and J. N. Tsitsiklis. 1989. *Parallel and Distributed Computation.* Englewood Cliffs, N.J.: Prentice-Hall.

Bhattacharya, R. N., and M. Majumdar. 1973. "Random Exchange Economies." *Journal of Economic Theory* 6: 37–67.

Binmore, K. 1992. *Fun and Games*. Lexington, Mass.: D. C. Heath and Company.

Binmore, K., and P. Dasgupta. 1987. *The Economics of Bargaining*. Oxford: Blackwell.

Booch, G. 1994. *Object-Oriented Analysis and Design with Applications*. 2d ed. Redwood City, Calif.: Benjamin/Cummings.

Bousquet, F. 1996. "Fishermen's Society." In *Simulating Societies*, edited by N. Gilbert and J. Doran. London: UCL Press.

Bousquet, F., C. Cambier, and P. Morand. 1994. "Distributed Artificial Intelligence and Object-Oriented Modelling of a Fishery." *Mathematical Computation Modelling* 20 (8): 97–107.

Boyd, R., and P. J. Richerson. 1985. *Culture and the Evolutionary Process*. Chicago: University of Chicago Press.

Boylan, R. D. 1991. "A Note on Epidemics in Heterogeneous Populations." *Mathematical Biosciences* 105: 133–37.

Brittain, J. A. 1977. *The Inheritance of Economic Status*. Brookings.

———. 1978. *Inheritance and the Inequality of Material Wealth*. Brookings.

Brooks, R., and P. Maes, eds. 1994. *Artificial Life IV*. MIT Press.

Builder, C., and S. Bankes. 1991. "Artificial Societies: A Concept for Basic Research on the Societal Impacts of Information Technology." RAND Report P-7740. Santa Monica, Calif.: RAND Corporation.

Busenberg, S., and P. van den Driessche. 1990. "Analysis of a Disease Transmission Model in a Population with Varying Size." *Journal of Mathematical Biology* 28: 257–70.

Buss, S., C. H. Papadimitriou, and J. N. Tsitsiklis. 1991. "On the Predictability of Coupled Automata." *Complex Systems* 5: 525–39.

Campbell, D. E. 1987. *Resource Allocation Mechanisms*. New York: Cambridge University Press.

Carley, K. 1991. "A Theory of Group Stability." *American Sociological Review* 56: 331–54.

Carley, K., and M. Prietula, eds. 1994. *Computational Organizational Theory*. Hillsdale, N.J.: Lawrence Erlbaum Associates.

Carley, K. M., *et al.* 1994. "Testing Alternative Models of Network Evolution." Working Paper. Carnegie Mellon University.

Carlson, J. A., and D. R. Pescatrice. 1980. "Persistent Price Distributions." *Journal of Economics and Business* 33: 21–27.

Casti, J. L. 1989. *Paradigms Lost*. Avon Books.

———. 1994. *Complexification: Explaining a Paradoxical World through the Science of Surprise*. Wiley.

Cavalli-Sforza, L. L., and M. W. Feldman. 1981. *Cultural Transmission and Evolution: A Quantitative Approach*. Princeton University Press.

Cohen, J. E. 1985. "Can Fitness Be Aggregated?" *American Naturalist* 125 (5): 716–29.

———. 1995. *How Many People Can the Earth Support?* Norton.

Cook, K. S., and M. Levi, eds. 1990. *The Limits of Rationality*. University of Chicago Press.

Cowen, T. 1989. "Are All Tastes Constant and Identical? A Critique of Stigler and Becker." *Journal of Economic Behavior and Organization* 11 (1): 127–35.

———. 1993. "The Scope and Limits of Preference Sovereignty." *Economics and Philosophy* 9: 253–69.

Crist, T. O., and J. W. Haefner. 1994. "Spatial Model of Movement and Foraging in Harvester Ants (Pogonomyrmex) (II): The Roles of Environment and Seed Dispersion." *Journal of Theoretical Biology* 166: 315–23.

Cusack, T. R., and R. J. Stoll. 1990. *Exploring Realpolitik: Probing International Relations Theory with Computer Simulation*. Boulder, Colo.: Lynne Rienner.

Dagum, C. 1990. "Gini Ratio." In *The New Palgrave Dictionary of Economics*, edited by J. Eatwell, M. Milgate, and P. Newman. New York: Stockton Press.

Danielson, P. 1992. *Artificial Morality: Virtuous Robots for Virtual Games*. New York: Routledge.

———, ed. 1996. *Modelling Rationality, Morality and Evolution*. New York: Oxford University Press.

Dawkins, R. 1976. *The Selfish Gene*. New York: Oxford University Press.

Derrick, W. R., and P. van den Driessche. 1993. "A Disease Transmission Model in a Nonconstant Population." *Journal of Mathematical Biology* 31 (5): 495–512.

Doolen, G. D., *et al.* eds. 1990. *Lattice Gas Methods for Partial Differential Equations*. Redwood City, Calif.: Addison-Wesley.

Doran, J., *et al.* 1994. "The EOS Project: Modelling Upper Palaeolithic Social Change." In *Simulating Societies: The Computer Simulation of Social Phenomena*, edited by N. Gilbert and J. Doran. London: Pitner Publishers.

Eatwell, J., M. Milgate, and P. Newman, eds. 1987. *The New Palgrave Dictionary of Economics*. New York: Stockton Press.

Eckalbar, J. 1984. "Money, Barter, and Convergence to the Competitive Allocation: Menger's Problem." *Journal of Economic Theory* 32 (2): 201–11.

———. 1986. "Bilateral Trade in a Monetized Pure Exchange Economy." *Economic Modelling* (April): 135–39.

Edelstein-Keshet, L. 1988. *Mathematical Models in Biology*. Birkhaüser Mathematics Series. Random House.

Eigen, M., and R. Winkler. 1981. *Laws of the Game: How the Principles of Nature Govern Chance*. Knopf.

Ellison, G. 1992. "Learning, Local Interaction, and Coordination." Working Paper. Harvard University, Department of Economics.

Epstein, J. M., and R. Axtell. 1996. "Artificial Societies and Generative Social Science." In *Proceedings of the First International Symposium on Artificial Life and*

Robotics, edited by M. Sugisaka. Oita, Japan: International Society for Artificial Life and Robotics.

Ermentrout, G. B., and L. Edelstein-Keshet. 1993. "Cellular Automata Approaches to Biological Modeling." *Journal of Theoretical Biology* 160: 97–113.

Feldman, A. 1973. "Bilateral Trading Processes, Pairwise Optimality, and Pareto Optimality." *Review of Economic Studies* 40 (4): 463–73.

Feldman, M. W., ed. 1989. *Mathematical Evolutionary Theory*. Princeton University Press.

Feldman, M. W., and L. L. Cavalli-Sforza. 1989. "On the Theory of Evolution under Genetic and Cultural Transmission with Application to the Lactose Absorption Problem." In *Mathematical Evolutionary Theory*, edited by M. W. Feldman. Princeton University Press.

Ferguson, R. B. 1992. "Tribal Warfare." *Scientific American* (January): 108–13.

Fisher, F. M. 1983. *Disequilibrium Foundations of Equilibrium Economics*. New York: Cambridge University Press.

Foley, D. K. 1994. "A Statistical Equilibrium Theory of Markets." *Journal of Economic Theory* 62: 321–45.

Föllmer, H. 1974. "Random Economies with Many Interacting Agents." *Journal of Mathematical Economics* 1 (1): 51–62.

Forrest, S., ed. 1991. *Emergent Computation: Self-Organizing, Collective, and Cooperative Phenomena in Nature and Artificial Computing Networks*. MIT Press.

Freedman, H. I., and Q. Hongshun. 1988. "Interactions Leading to Persistence in Predator-Prey Systems with Group Defence." *Bulletin of Mathematical Biology* 50 (5): 517–30.

Freedman, H. I., and G. S. Wolkowicz. 1986. "Predator-Prey Systems with Group Defence: The Paradox of Enrichment Revisited." *Bulletin of Mathematical Biology* 48: (5/6): 493–508.

Friedman, D. 1979. "Money-Mediated Disequilibrium Processes in a Pure Exchange Economy." *Journal of Mathematical Economics* 6: 463–73.

Gale, D. 1986a. "Bargaining and Competition Part I: Characterization." *Econometrica* 54 (4): 785–806.

———. 1986b. "Bargaining and Competition Part II: Existence." *Econometrica* 54 (4): 807–18.

Gao, L. Q., and H. W. Hethcote. 1992. "Disease Transmission Models with Density-Dependent Demographics." *Journal of Mathematical Biology* 30: 717–31.

Garman, M. B. 1976. "Market Microstructure." *Journal of Financial Economics* 3: 257–75.

Gasser, L., and M. N. Huhns. 1989. *Distributed Artificial Intelligence*. Vol. 2. San Mateo, Calif.: Morgan Kaufmann.

Gilbert, N., and J. Doran, eds. 1994. *Simulating Societies: The Computer Simulation of Social Phenomena*. London: UCL Press.

Gilbert, N., and R. Conte, eds. 1995. *Artificial Societies: The Computer Simulation of Social Life*. London: UCL Press.

Glance, N. S., and B. A. Huberman. 1993. "The Outbreak of Cooperation." *Journal of Mathematical Sociology* 17 (4): 281–302.

———. 1994a. "The Dynamics of Social Dilemmas." *Scientific American* (March): 76–81.

———. 1994b. "Social Dilemmas and Fluid Organizations." In *Computational Organization Theory*, edited by K. M. Carley and M. J. Prietula. Hillsdale, N.J.: Lawrence Erlbaum Associates.

Goldman, S. M., and R. M. Starr. 1982. "Pairwise, t-wise and Pareto Optimalities." *Econometrica* 50 (3): 593–606.

Goodin, R. E. 1990. "De Gustibus Non Est Explanadum." In *The Limits of Rationality*, edited by K. S. Cook and M. Levi. University of Chicago Press.

Gueron, S., and S. A. Levin. 1993. "Self-Organization of Front Patterns in Large Wildebeest Herds." *Journal of Theoretical Biology* 165: 541–52.

———. 1994. "The Dynamics of Group Formation." Working Paper. Princeton University, Department of Ecology and Evolutionary Biology.

Gueron, S., S. A. Levin, and D. I. Rubenstein. 1993. "The Dynamics of Mammalian Herds: From Individuals to Aggregations." Working Paper. Princeton University, Department of Ecology and Evolutionary Biology.

Guesnerie, R., and J.-J. Laffont. 1978. "Advantageous Reallocations of Initial Resources." *Econometrica* 46 (4): 835–41.

Gumerman, G. J., and T. A. Kohler. 1996. "Creating Alternative Cultural Histories in the Prehistoric Southwest: Agent-based Modeling in Archaeology." Working Paper 96-03-007. Santa Fe, N.M.: Santa Fe Institute.

Gutowitz, H., ed. 1991. *Cellular Automata: Theory and Experiment*. MIT Press.

Haefner, J. W., and T. O. Crist. 1994. "Spatial Model of Movement and Foraging in Harvester Ants (Pogonomyrmex) (I): The Roles of Memory and Communication." *Journal of Theoretical Biology* 166: 299–313.

Hahn, F. 1962. "On the Stability of Pure Exchange Equilibrium." *International Economic Review* 3 (2): 206–13.

———. 1981. "Reflections on the Invisible Hand." *Lloyds Bank Review* 144: 1–21.

———. 1982. "Stability." In *Handbook of Mathematical Economics*, vol. 2, edited by K. J. Arrow and M. D. Intriligator. New York: North-Holland.

Hastings, A., and K. Higgins. 1994. "Persistence of Transients in Spatially Structured Ecological Models." *Science* 263 (February 25): 1133–36.

Hausman, D. M. 1992. *The Inexact and Separate Science of Economics*. New York: Cambridge University Press.

Herz, A. V. M. 1993. "Collective Phenomena in Spatially Extended Evolutionary Games." Working Paper. University of Illinois, Beckman Institute.

Hey, J. D. 1974. "Price Adjustment in an Atomistic Market." *Journal of Economic Theory* 8: 483–99.

Hicks, J. R. 1946. *Value and Capital.* New York: Oxford University Press.

Hildebrand, W., and A. Kirman. 1988. *Equilibrium Analysis: Variations on Themes by Edgeworth and Walras.* New York: Elsevier Science Publishing.

Hirsch, M. D., C. H. Papadimitriou, and S. A. Vavasis. 1989. "Exponential Lower Bounds for Finding Brouwer Fixed Points." *Journal of Complexity* 5: 379–416.

Holland, J. 1992. *Adaptation in Natural and Artificial Systems: An Introductory Analysis with Applications to Biology, Control, and Artificial Intelligence.* 2d ed. MIT Press.

———. 1993. "The Effects of Labels (Tags) on Social Interactions." Working Paper 93-10-064. Santa Fe, N.M.: Santa Fe Institute.

Holland, J., and J. Miller. 1991. "Artificial Adaptive Agents in Economic Theory." *American Economic Review, Papers and Proceedings* 81 (2): 365–70.

Homer-Dixon, T. F. 1991. "On the Threshold: Environmental Changes as Causes of Acute Conflict." *International Security* 16 (2): 76–116.

———. 1994. "Environmental Scarcities and Violent Conflict: Evidence from Cases." *International Security* 19: (3): 5–40.

Huberman, B. A. 1988. *The Ecology of Computation.* New York: North-Holland.

Huberman, B. A., and N. S. Glance. 1993. "Evolutionary Games and Computer Simulations." *Proceedings of the National Academy of Sciences, USA* 90 (August): 7716–18.

———. 1996. "Beliefs and Cooperation." In *Modelling Rationality, Morality and Evolution,* edited by P. Danielson. New York: Oxford University Press.

Huberman, B. A., and T. Hogg. 1995. "Communities of Practice: Performance and Evolution." *Computational and Mathematical Organization Theory* 1 (1): 73–92.

Hurwicz, L., R. Radner, and S. Reiter. 1975a. "A Stochastic Decentralized Resource Allocation Process: Part I." *Econometrica* 43 (2): 187–221.

———. 1975b. "A Stochastic Decentralized Resource Allocation Process: Part II." *Econometrica* 43 (3): 363–93.

Ioannides, Y. M. 1975. "Market Allocation through Search: Equilibrium Adjustment and Price Dispersion." *Journal of Economic Theory* 11: 247–62.

Jacobs, J. 1992. *Systems of Survival: A Dialogue on the Moral Foundations of Commerce and Politics.* Random House.

Jen, E., ed. 1990. *1989 Lectures in Complex Systems.* Redwood City, Calif.: Addison-Wesley.

Kakwani, N. 1990. "Lorenz Curve." In *The New Palgrave Dictionary of Economics,* edited by J. Eatwell, M. Milgate, and P. Newman. New York: Stockton Press.

Kaniovski, Yu. 1994. "Technological Adoption and Urn Processes." Lecture at International Institute for Applied Systems Analysis (IIASA) Colloquium on Evolutionary Economics. Laxenburg, Austria.

Karni, E., and D. Schmeidler. 1989. "Fixed Preferences and Changing Tastes." *American Economic Review* 80 (2): 262–67.

Kauffman, S. 1988. "The Evolution of Economic Webs." In *The Economy as an Evolving Complex System*, edited by P. W. Anderson, K. J. Arrow, and D. Pines. Redwood City, Calif.: Addison-Wesley.

Keisler, H. J. 1986. "A Price Adjustment Model with Infinitesimal Traders." In *Models of Economic Dynamics*, edited by H. F. Sonnenschein. New York: Springer-Verlag.

———. 1992. "A Law of Large Numbers for Fast Price Adjustment." *Transactions of the American Mathematical Society* 332 (1): 1–51.

———. 1995. "Approximate Tétonnement Processes." *Economic Theory* 5: 127–73.

———. 1996. "Getting to a Competitive Equilibrium." *Econometrica* 64 (1): 29–49.

Kiefer, N. M., Z. Ye, and M. Y. An. 1993. "A Dynamic Model of Local and Global Interactions among Economic Agents." Working Paper. Cornell University, Department of Economics.

Kirman, A. 1989. "The Intrinsic Limits of Modern Economic Theory: The Emperor Has No Clothes." *The Economic Journal* 99: 126–39.

———. 1990. "Pareto as an Economist." In *The New Palgrave Dictionary of Economics*, edited by J. Eatwell, M. Milgate, and P. Newman. New York: Stockton Press.

———. 1992. "Whom or What Does the Representative Agent Represent." *Journal of Economic Perspectives* 6 (2): 117–36.

———. 1993. "Ants, Rationality, and Recruitment." *Quarterly Journal of Economics* 8: 137–56.

———. 1994. "Economies with Interacting Agents." Working Paper 94-05-030. Santa Fe, N.M.: Santa Fe Institute.

Kitano, H., and J. A. Hendler. 1994. *Massively Parallel Artificial Intelligence*. Menlo Park, Calif.: AAAI Press/MIT Press.

Kiyotaki, N., and R. Wright. 1989. "On Money as a Medium of Exchange." *Journal of Political Economy* 97 (4): 927–54.

———. 1991. "A Contribution to the Pure Theory of Money." *Journal of Economic Theory* 53: 215–35.

Kochen, M., ed. 1989. *The Small World*. Norwood, N.J.: Ablex Publishing Corporation.

Kollman, K., J. H. Miller, and S. E. Page. 1992. "Adaptive Parties in Spatial Elections." *American Political Science Review* 86: 929–37.

———. 1994. "The Comparison of Political Institutions in a Tiebout Model." Working Paper 95-04-045. Santa Fe, N.M.: Santa Fe Institute.

Koza, J. 1992. *Genetic Programming: On the Programming of Machines by Means of Natural Selection*. MIT Press.

———. 1994. *Genetic Programming II: Automatic Discovery of Reusable Programs*. MIT Press.

Kreps, D. M. 1990. *A Course in Microeconomic Theory*. Princeton University Press.

Krugman, P. 1994. *Peddling Prosperity*. Norton.

———. 1996. *The Self-Organizing Economy*. Cambridge, Mass.: Blackwell.

Lane, D. 1993. "Artificial Worlds and Economics." Parts 1 and 2. *Journal of Evolutionary Economics* 3: 89–107, 177–97.

Langton, C. G., ed. 1989. *Artificial Life*. Redwood City, Calif.: Addison-Wesley.

———. 1992. *Artificial Life II Video Proceedings*. Redwood City, Calif.: Addison-Wesley.

———. 1994. *Artificial Life III*. Redwood City, Calif.: Addison-Wesley.

Langton, C. G., *et al.* eds. 1992. *Artificial Life II*. Redwood City, Calif.: Addison-Wesley.

Lengwiler, Y. H. 1994. *Bilateral Economies: A Game-Theoretic Analysis of General Economic Equilibrium*. Ph.D. dissertation. University of St. Gallen, Switzerland.

Lindgren, K., 1992. "Evolutionary Phenomena in Simple Dynamics." In *Artificial Life II*, edited by C. G. Langton *et al.* Redwood City, Calif.: Addison-Wesley.

Lindgren, K., and M. G. Nordahl. 1994. "Artificial Food Webs." In *Artificial Life III*, edited by C. G. Langton. Redwood City, Calif.: Addison-Wesley.

Linhart, P. B., R. Radner, and M. A. Satterthwaite. 1992. *Bargaining with Incomplete Information*. New York: Academic Press.

McClelland, J. L., and D. E. Rumelhart. 1986. *Parallel Distributed Processing: Explorations in the Microstructure of Cognition*. Vol. 2. MIT Press.

McNeill, W. H., 1976. *Plagues and Peoples*. Anchor Press/Doubleday.

Madden, P. J. 1976. "A Theorem on Decentralized Exchange." *Econometrica* 44 (4): 787–91.

Maes, P., ed. 1990. *Designing Autonomous Agents: Theory and Practice from Biology to Engineering and Back*. MIT Press.

Marimon, R., E. McGrattan, and T. J. Sargent. 1990. "Money as a Medium of Exchange in an Economy with Artificially Intelligent Agents." *Journal of Economic Dynamics and Control* 14: 329–73.

Marks, R. E. 1992. "Breeding Hybrid Strategies: Optimal Behavior for Oligopolists." *Journal of Evolutionary Economics* 2: 17–38.

May, R. M., and R. M. Anderson. 1984. "Spatial Heterogeneity and the Design of Immunization Programs." *Mathematical Biosciences* 72 (1): 83–111.

Mendelson, H. 1985. "Random Competitive Exchange: Price Distributions and Gains from Trade." *Journal of Economic Theory* 37: 254–80.

Menger, K. 1892. "On the Origin of Money." *Economic Journal* 2: 239–55.

Miller, J. H. 1989. "The Coevolution of Automata in the Repeated Prisoner's Dilemma." Working Paper 89-003. Santa Fe, N.M.: Santa Fe Institute.

Miller, M. S., and K. E. Drexler. 1988. "Markets and Computation: Agoric Open Systems." In *The Ecology of Computation*, edited by B. A. Huberman. New York: North-Holland.

Mukherji, A. 1974. "The Edgeworth-Uzawa Barter Stabilizes Prices." *International Economic Review* 15 (1): 236–41.

Murray, J. D. 1989. *Mathematical Biology.* New York: Springer-Verlag.

Nagel, K., and E. Raschke. 1992. "Self-Organized Criticality in Cloud Formation?" *Physica A* 182: 519–31.

Nagel, K., and S. Rasmussen. 1994. "Traffic on the Edge of Chaos." Working Paper 94-06-032. Santa Fe, N.M.: Santa Fe Institute.

Negishi, T. 1961. "On the Formation of Prices." *International Economic Review* 2 (1): 122–26.

Newell, A., and H. Simon. 1972. *Human Problem Solving.* Englewood Cliffs, N.J.: Prentice-Hall.

Nold, A. 1980. "Heterogeneity in Disease-Transmission Modeling." *Mathematical Biosciences* 52 (3/4): 227–40.

Nordhaus, W. D. 1992. "Lethal Model 2: The Limits to Growth Revisited." *Brookings Papers on Economic Activity: 2:* 1–59.

Norman, A. L. 1987. "A Theory of Monetary Exchange." *Review of Economic Studies* 54 (179): 499–517.

Nozick, R. 1974. *Anarchy, State and Utopia.* Basic Books.

———. 1994. "Invisible-Hand Explanations." *American Economic Review, Papers and Proceedings* 84 (2): 314–18.

Oelschläger, K. 1992. "The Spread of a Parasitic Infection in a Spatially Distributed Host Population." *Journal of Mathematical Biology* 30 (4): 321–54.

Orcutt, G. H., *et al.* 1961. *Microanalysis of Socioeconomic Systems: A Simulation Study.* Harper and Row.

Osborne, M. J., and A. Rubinstein. 1990. *Bargaining and Markets.* San Diego, Calif.: Academic Press.

Ostrom, E. 1990. *Governing the Commons: The Evolution of Institutions for Collective Action.* New York: Cambridge University Press.

Ostrom, E., R. Gardner, and J. Walker. 1994. *Rules, Games, and Common-Pool Resources.* University of Michigan Press.

Ostroy, J. M., and R. M. Starr. 1974. "Money and the Decentralization of Exchange." *Econometrica* 42 (6): 1093–13.

———. 1990. "The Transactions Role of Money." In *Handbook of Monetary Economics,* vol. 1, edited by B. M. Friedman and F. H. Hahn. New York: North-Holland.

Packard, N. 1989. "Intrinsic Adaptation in a Simple Model for Evolution." In *Artificial Life,* edited by C. G. Langton. Redwood City, Calif.: Addison-Wesley.

Papadimitriou, C. H. 1994. "On the Complexity of the Parity Argument and Other Inefficient Proofs of Existence." *Journal of Computer and System Sciences* 49: 498–532.

Papageorgiou, Y. Y., and T. R. Smith. 1983. "Agglomeration as Local Instability of Spatially Uniform Steady-States." *Econometrica* 51 (4): 1109–19.

Peleg, B., and M. E. Yaari. 1973. "On the Existence of a Consistent Course of Action When Tastes Are Changing." *Review of Economic Studies* 40: 391–401.

Perelson, A. S., ed. 1988. *Theoretical Immunology.* 2 vols. Redwood City, Calif.: Addison-Wesley.

———. 1989. "Theoretical Immunology." In *1989 Lectures in Complex Systems,* edited by E. Jen. Redwood City, Calif.: Addison-Wesley.

Persky, J. 1992. "Retrospectives: Pareto's Law." *Journal of Economic Perspectives* 6 (2): 767–73.

Pratt, J. W., D. A. Wise, and R. Zeckhauser. 1979. "Price Differences in Almost Competitive Markets." *Quarterly Journal of Economics* 93: 189–211.

Radner, R. 1982. "Equilibrium under Uncertainty." In *Handbook of Mathematical Economics,* vol. 2, edited by K. J. Arrow and M. D. Intriligator. New York: North-Holland.

Rapoport, A., and Y. Yuan. 1989. "Some Aspects of Epidemics and Social Nets." In *The Small World,* edited by M. Kochen. Norwood, N.J.: Ablex Publishing.

Reinganum, J. F. 1979. "A Simple Model of Equilibrium Price Dispersion." *Journal of Political Economy* 87 (4): 851–58.

Resnick, M. 1994. *Turtles, Termites, and Traffic Jams: Explorations in Massively Parallel Microworlds.* MIT Press.

Rothschild, E. 1994. "Adam Smith and the Invisible Hand." *American Economic Review, Papers and Proceedings* 84 (2): 319–22.

Rumelhart, D. E., and J. L. McClelland. 1986. *Parallel Distributed Processing: Explorations in the Microstructure of Cognition.* Vol. 1. MIT Press.

Sanil, A., D. Banks, and K. Carley. 1994. "Models for Evolving Fixed Node Networks: Model Fitting and Model Testing." Working Paper. Carnegie Mellon University, Department of Social and Decision Sciences.

Sato, K., and Iwasa, Y. 1993. "Modeling of Wave Regeneration in Subalpine Abies Forests: Population Dynamics with Spatial Structure." *Ecology* 74 (5): 1538–50.

Scarf, H. 1973. *The Computation of Economic Equilibria.* Yale University Press.

Schelling, T. C. 1969. "Models of Segregation." *American Economic Review, Papers and Proceedings* 59 (2): 488–93.

———. 1971a. "Dynamic Models of Segregation." *Journal of Mathematical Sociology* 1: 143–86.

———. 1971b. "On the Ecology of Micromotives." *The Public Interest* 25 (Fall): 61–98.

———. 1978. *Micromotives and Macrobehavior.* Norton.

Scott, J. 1992. *Social Network Analysis: A Handbook.* New York: Sage.

Sedgewick, R. 1983. *Algorithms.* Reading, Mass.: Addison-Wesley.

Shakespeare, W. 1917. *Much Ado About Nothing.* Yale University Press.

Sigmund, K. 1993. *Games of Life: Explorations in Ecology, Evolution, and Behaviour.* New York: Oxford University Press.

Simon, H. 1981. "The Architecture of Complexity." In *The Sciences of the Artificial.* 2d ed. MIT Press.

———. 1987. "Giving the Soft Sciences a Hard Sell." *Boston Globe* (3 May).

————. 1990. "Prediction and Prescription in Systems Modeling." *Operations Research* 38 (1): 7–14.

Smale, S. 1976. "Exchange Processes with Price Adjustment." *Journal of Mathematical Economics* 3 (3): 211–26.

Smith, A. 1976. *An Inquiry into the Nature and Causes of the Wealth of Nations.* Oxford: Oxford University Press (originally published in 1776).

Sober, E., ed. 1994. *Conceptual Issues in Evolutionary Biology.* 2d ed. MIT Press.

Stacchetti, E. 1985. "Analysis of a Dynamic, Decentralized Exchange Economy." *Journal of Mathematical Economics* 14: 241–59.

Starr, R. M. 1976. "Decentralized Nonmonetary Trade." *Econometrica* 44 (5): 1087–89.

Steinbruner, J. 1974. *The Cybernetic Theory of Decision. New Dimensions of Political Analysis.* Princeton University Press.

Steindl, J. 1990. "Pareto Distribution." In *The New Palgrave Dictionary of Economics,* edited by J. Eatwell, M. Milgate, and P. Newman. New York: Stockton Press.

Stigler, G. J., and G. S. Becker. 1977. "De Gustibus Non Est Disputandum." *American Economic Review* 67 (2): 76–90.

Stokey, N. L., and R. E. Lucas. 1989. *Recursive Methods in Economic Dynamics.* Harvard University Press.

Takayasu, H., *et al.* 1992. "Statistical Properties of Deterministic Threshold Elements: The Case of Market Price." *Physica A* 184: 127–34.

Tesfatsion, L. 1995. "A Trade Network Game with Endogenous Partner Selection." Economic Report 36. Iowa State University, Department of Economics.

Toffoli, T., and N. Margolus. 1987. *Cellular Automata Machines: A New Environment for Modeling.* MIT Press.

Uzawa, H. 1962. "On the Stability of Edgeworth's Barter Process." *International Economic Review* 3 (2): 218–32.

Vandell, K. D., and B. Harrison. 1978. "Racial Transition among Neighborhoods: A Simulation Model Incorporating Institutional Parameters." *Journal of Urban Economics* 5: 441–70.

Varian, H. 1984. *Microeconomic Analysis.* 2d ed. Norton.

Vickers, G. T., V. C. L. Hutson, and C. J. Budd. 1993. "Spatial Patterns in Population Conflicts." *Journal of Mathematical Biology* 31 (4): 411–30.

von Neumann, J. 1966. *Theory of Self-Reproducing Automata.* Edited by A. W. Burks. University of Illinois Press.

Vriend, N. 1995. "Self Organization of Markets: An Example of a Computational Approach." *Journal of Computational Economics* 8 (3): 205–31.

Walker, M. 1984. "A Simple Auctioneerless Mechanism with Walrasian Properties." *Journal of Economics Theory* 32: 111–27.

Wallace, R. 1991. "Social Disintegration and the Spread of AIDS: Thresholds for Propagation along 'Sociogeographic' Networks." *Social Science Media* 33 (10): 1155–62.

Werner, G. M., and M. G. Dyer. 1994. "BioLand: A Massively Parallel Simulation Environment for Evolving Distributed Forms of Intelligent Behavior." In *Massively Parallel Artificial Intelligence*, edited by H. Kitano and J. A. Handler. Menlo Park, Calif.: AAAI Press/MIT Press.

Wiener, N. 1961. *Cybernetics; Or, Control and Communication in the Animal and the Machine.* 2d ed. MIT Press.

Wolff, R. S., and L. Yeager. 1993. *Visualization of Natural Phenomena.* Santa Clara, Calif.: TELOS.

Wolfram, S. 1994. *Cellular Automata and Complexity.* Reading, Mass.: Addison-Wesley.

Yeager, L. 1994. "Computational Genetics, Physiology, Metabolism, Neural Systems, Learning, Vision, and Behavior or PolyWorld: Life in a New Context." In *Artificial Life III*, edited by C. G. Langton. Redwood City, Calif.: Addison-Wesley.

Youssefmir, M., and B. A. Huberman. 1995. "Clustered Volatility in Multiagent Dynamics." Working Paper 95-05-051. Santa Fe, N.M.: Santa Fe Institute. Forthcoming in *Journal of Economic Behavior and Organization.*

Index

Aaron, H., 1*n*3
Ackley, D.H., 19*n*22, 63*n*8, 163*n*6
Agent-based modeling. *See* Model-building
Agents: data fields/instance variables, 5, 23*n*5; definition and use of, 4, 15, 23-25; evolution of, 18-19, 32; movement and migration of, 26-30, 42-45, 46, 48-51, 98-100, 140; neoclassical and non-neoclassical, 108-26; preferences of, 11, 124-26; procedures/methods, 5; social networks, 7-8, 12-13, 37-41, 68, 70-71; spread of infectious diseases and, 13-14; trade and, 12-13, 94-137; tribes, 82; wealth and holdings of, 24, 25, 32-36, 97-98; welfare of, 97-98, 104-05, 113-14, 116, 123, 124-25. *See also* Artificial society models; Combat and conflict; Cultural processes; Genetic factors; Life-span; Rules; Sexual reproduction; Sugarscape Model
Albin, P., 3, 102*n*11, 104
ALife, 14, 18-20
Anderson, R.M., 142*n*12, 144*n*13
Animations and time series: age and life-span, 58, 67, 122, 158, 160, 161; carrying capacity, 31, 112; combat and conflict, 84, 85, 87, 88, 89, 91; credit evolution, 134, 162; cultural and tag-flipping dynamics, 75, 76, 77, 91, 159; disease processes, 148, 149, 151, 163; evolution of artificial society, 155-163; foresight evolution, 130; genetic factors, 31, 61, 67, 68, 112; Lorenz Curve and Gini Coefficient, 38, 69, 123,

157; migration, movement, and hibernation, 43, 46, 49, 100; neighbors and networks, 41, 70, 80, 132, 134, 155-57, 167-69, 171; pollution, 49, 128; population, 31, 58, 64-67, 157; realization of proto-history, 92; Ring World, 173-74; societal evolution, 27, 29, 41, 60, 62; trade and prices, 109, 110, 115, 118, 119, 121, 122, 124-28, 132, 156-57; waves, 43, 88, 89; wealth evolution, 34, 155
Arifovic, J., 3
Arrow, K., 12*n*30, 102*n*11, 112*n*30, 137*n*60
Arthur, W.B., 3, 18, 74*n*22, 144*n*14, 162
Artificial society models: analysis of, 176-77; defining features, 6, 19*n*23; economies in, 135; markets in, 10-12; mathematical epidemiology in, 13-14; as a parallel computer, 13; rules in, 162, 163-64; software engineering aspects of, 179-80; and traditional models compared, 14-17, 66-67; use and goals of, 3-4, 14, 19-20, 36, 37, 52-53, 82, 95, 129, 153, 164-65, 177-78. *See also* Ring World; Model-building; Rules; Sugarscape Model
Ashby, W.R., 2
Axelrod, R., 3, 18*n*21, 71*n*15
Axtell, R.J., 20*nn*26-27, 71*n*15, 177*n*14, 178*n*18

Bak, P., 18
Bankes, S., 4*n*7
Becker, G.S., 124*n*43
Behavior. *See* Rules